# Cornucopia

## New and Selected Poems
### 1975 – 2002

ALSO BY MOLLY PEACOCK

POETRY

*And Live Apart*

*Raw Heaven*

*Take Heart*

*Original Love*

NONFICTION

*Paradise, Piece by Piece*

*How to Read a Poem and Start a Poetry Circle*

COEDITOR

*Poetry in Motion: 100 Poems from the Buses and Subways*

EDITOR

*The Private I: Privacy in a Public World*

# MOLLY PEACOCK

# *Cornucopia*

## NEW AND SELECTED POEMS

## 1975 – 2002

W. W. NORTON & COMPANY
*New York • London*

For information about permission to reproduce selections from
this book, write to Permissions, W. W. Norton & Company, Inc.,
500 Fifth Avenue, New York, NY 10110

The text of this book is composed in Bembo
with the display set in Cochin
Desktop composition by Tom Ernst
Manufacturing by Courier Westford
Book design by Julia Druskin

Library of Congress Cataloging-in-Publication Data
Peacock, Molly, date.
  Cornucopia : new & selected poems, 1975–2002 / by Molly Peacock.
    p. cm.
    Includes index.
  **ISBN 0-393-05123-4**
    I. Title
PS3566.E15 C67 2002
811'.54—dc21

2002022884

W. W. Norton & Company, Inc., 500 Fifth Avenue, New York, N.Y. 10110
www.wwnorton.com

W. W. Norton & Company Ltd., Castle House, 75/76 Wells Street,
London W1T 3QT

1 2 3 4 5 6 7 8 9 0

*For Michael Groden*

# Contents

FROM *And Live Apart* (1980)

FROM *Raw Heaven* (1984)

FROM *Take Heart (1989)*

FROM *Original Love (1995)*

*First Love*

## Mother Love

## Friends and a Lover

# *Acknowledgments*

Although the poems in this collection were published in book form beginning in 1980, the earliest poem, "Nightwake," was published in 1975 in *The Ohio Review*.

Poems in this volume have appeared in the following books:

*And Live Apart,* University of Missouri Press, 1980
*Raw Heaven,* Random House, 1984
*Take Heart,* Random House, 1989
*Original Love,* W. W. Norton & Company, 1995

The poems in *The Land of the Shí: New Poems 2002* have appeared (often in earlier versions, and sometimes with different titles) in the following anthologies and literary journals:

*Barrow Street* ("Ash Wednesday" and "Lexington Avenue Muse Dog"), *Boulevard* ("Nude at a Dressing Table" and "The Umbrella"), *The Cortland Review* ("Diary of Our Day in Painting Titles"), *Intimate Kisses: The Poetry of Sexual Pleasure* ("A Love Koan"), *KGB Bar Anthology* ("Breakfast with Cats"), *line-up* ("Couple Sharing a Peach"), *Poetry* ("A Favor of Love"), *Poetry After 9-11: An Anthology of New York Poets* ("The Land of the Shí"), *poetrybay.com* ("Refusal"), *Rattapallax* ("Conversation"), *Spirituality and Health* ("The Soul House"), *River*

*Styx* ("The Parsley Ship"), *TriQuarterly* ("Repair"), and *Van Gogh's Ear—Paris* ("Tan Oval Head Leaning Toward Tiny Brown Oval Shell").

With great pleasure I thank Carol Houck Smith, Richard Howard, Jonathan Galassi, Phillis Levin, Joan Stein, Georgianna Orsini, and Kathleen Anderson who have long believed in my work and encouraged me.

To the cover designer, Julie Metz, and to Jennifer Eiss, my gratitude.

# The Land of the Shí

## NEW POEMS 2002

The Land of the Shí (also spelled sidhe, sidh, or sí)
three times beguiles, first in meaning, then in sound,
and last in how we go there. The Land is also known
as Tir na n-Og, the Land of the Ever Young; the
Celtic shí flirts with "she"; and best of all, the writer
James Stephens tells us to get there by stopping, not
by going. Standing exactly where you are, the air
suddenly intensifies, and you are in another world.
In his *Irish Fairy Tales*, Stephens makes the shí the
grounds under which the banished faeries were
supposed to live, into a kind of Celtic zen, but as
well as being alive in the moment, you
are truly alive in a place.

# A FAVOR OF LOVE

"Thank you for making this sacrifice,"
I say to my husband as I run to Kim's market.
Never mind what the sacrifice is.
Sacrifices between husbands and wives are private,
and fill a person with simple, healing water.
Kim's buzzes with Sunday night customers
as into the plastic basket go
watercress, asparagus, garlic, pecans
when a girl throws herself through the plastic door flaps
tears streaming down her face while her boyfriend
catapults past the troughs of oranges screaming,
*Water! Water!*
And Mr. Kim peers down his quizzical nose
and Mrs. Kim stands in mountain pose

openly hating the girl for dying of an overdose
among the lemons, mangoes, papayas, and limes
of the country of her family's origins
plunging among the plums and dying there
the color of a plum beneath her dark hair
for the girl is turning purple.
From the back of the store by the water the boyfriend
shouts that she's swallowed a lollipop head.
Now she is almost the color of an eggplant,
and young Mr. Kim by the register is asking her,
"Should I call 911?" in a pleasant, insistent whisper,
"Should I call 911?"
Big sound should boom from her, but only a bubble
squeaks at her lips. "Call 911!" I speak for her

raising my woollen arm, aiming for her
shoulder blades where I whack, whack her again,
and no lollipop pops out. But sound bellows out!
Like idiots everywhere, her boyfriend shouts
*Calm down, Calm down,* forcing water into her throat,
which must help dissolve the candy my backslap dislodged.
"Where's that Choking Victims poster you're supposed to hang?"
the boyfriend demands of young Mr. Kim.
"I'll cancel 911," he says.
"Where is that lady?" the sobbing girl is asking.
*Right here,* I say, *I am right here behind you.*
I am putting endive in my basket.
As she grabs me in a bear hug,
her face has a human color


and it is a hard face, strong and horsey.
"Oh Mommy!" she shouts.
As my sister was dying she called me Mommy.
I stand in a mountain pose,
and she smiles up from a pile of plastic baskets.
"My name is Marisol!" she spouts.
*My name is Molly!*
(I'm afraid she might hear those *l*'s as *m*'s.)
"Thank you for saving my life!"
*Now don't eat any more lollipops,* I say mommily,
closing the cosmic circle begun at breakfast
when my husband made the promise I won't reveal.
Grown human beings making sacrifices
return to the universe a favor of love.

# A LOVE KOAN

I love your face when we are making love,
like the living stones I was shocked to find
were plants, were succulents, were members of
a live species, although they looked like blind
unblinking pebbles, unleaved and ungreen
and ungrown, so of course they were unknown
to me, as your face is, beside me—for
we have gotten ourselves in a love koan
as if we were a shunga print born
up through Western life, torsos aslant, but
legs lifted (will we ever again find
a position so side by side?)—brows cut
into angles acutely unknown to me, eyes green
above the brown mouth's living O, a species find.

## THE LAND OF THE SHÍ

The Land of the Shí
is the same land we inhabit only
the heart beats more insistently.
All green is Green, you'd say,
everything gray is itself, only more Gray.
You can stand in the place you're standing in
and enter the Land of the Shí.
Even the rain which rains on Avenue A
in the Land of the Shí rains silkier
and you, parched in New York City,
become more deeply quenched.
The ear of a pug who waits at the light
is silkier and more pugly.
Money is exactly the same rate,

except that every dollar has individual weight,
and a New York City kiss
in the Land of the Shí is palpable as sculpted flesh.
It is the beautiful place we yearned for as boys and girls,
the Land of Faery one needs only mental transport for.
Oh brown institutional housing of the He,
vanish beneath, vanish beneath
as detritus into running water. . . .
That pug in his red rainboots at the corner
now breathes free through two little nostrils cleared
in the Land of Faery, where the dry cleaners is still
on the corner across from the 24-hr Deli,
and a lost thought appears for a moment
as a tender face on a penny.

# LEXINGTON AVENUE MUSEDOG

Somewhere in the Land of the Shí
a Passionate One is turned into a dog,
feral and furious, and this dog bites
Lexington Avenue with ferocious cold.
The building on Madison and 88th stands
its stoic stance: *"No Dog of Wind will gust*
*so much as a toothcut in my canopy!"*
Patted by the warm palm of its lobby,
scooped up like toy dogs into the elevator
invisibly operated by the doorman,
Mike and I ride up, up, to order Sunday takeout
from the kitchen of Ajax the brindle whippet,
supervisor of Philip and Phoebe, and of Betsy,
teary-eyed from a silent Battle with the Dog
of her own passionate nature which
she has run from, and then with, and then to,
inventing her own Land of the She.

Ajax, glow-eyed, her life-size Musedog, observes
her terrors from his pillows under her desk,
and, when we finish our dinner, dons his sweater
and prances to the elevator, shivering.
Mike and I, with Betsy leashed to Ajax,
shake in the blast of Id Canine Fury Breath
as the palm of the lobby flips us into 88th Street
as if from ordinary life into the Land of the Shí
which is everywhere since it is everywhere ordinary life is.
"Let's hurry," I whine. "I've only got my raincoat on!"
Mike, leashed to a Great Writer, wears his James Joyce cap.
Joyce's designee for the Ajax who would finish the *Wake?*

Folksy little James Stephens who invented the Land of the Shí
in his tales of faery, thin little sweaters of love,
all Joyce had to protect him, all anyone has,
as the Passionate One, lost to Itself,
howls, transmogrified, through the Land of the City.

# ASH WEDNESDAY, HURRYING EASTWARD

A girl with a dirty forehead
in the blast of light on lower Fifth Avenue
reminds me: Ash Wednesday!
My body rushes to Ascension Church
only to find it padlocked, a chain bunched
into a heart-shaped lump on the wrought-iron gate.
Damn! I should have gone to yoga after all.
A spring light pink as a girl's tongue
licks the spire of Grace Church three blocks east,
and the doors of Grace fling open to its
gothic waffle cone interior where
I almost run down the aisle genuflecting
though I cannot slip the hellish pew-latch open.

When it finally springs, my skeleton,
who doesn't know how to pray, poses as
a worried soul lounging half-bored over the pew
and chatters: *I don't feel like atoning! I am so!*
*I am so worthy to pick up the crumbs under your table,*
while the verger snuffs the candles inside
the ventricles of Grace. Damn! I've missed the ashes.

But before I run to meet my friend Corrine
and her daughter Camille at Haveli Indian Restaurant,
I can't resist a moment in this pew
where there is not one thing to do
but feel all excess drain down to a heartbeat
as the altar frou-frou of stained glass crosses
darkens. I stop posing, and my soul slips in.

Why bother to pretend?
We tear our nan into tongues to scoop our saag,
delighting teenage Camille by dissecting
the heart of an old love affair I had.
*He wants to meet you again,*
Corrine conveys. I am thrilled!
Not at the prospect of the actual lunch
which, as I imagine my husband's shocked face,
may never happen, but at, in stained glass terms,
the annealing. Hell? Being locked out
—there were actual chains around that wrought-iron fence
of the first church I went to. Heavenly love?
the thought of being wanted still.

# NUDE AT A DRESSING TABLE

A marmalade tabby ate her ring,
a ruby flower from Amsterdam, and then
an insistent lover went driving
over her amber brooch. Brooch broken,
ring lost. One jade earring flew from her ear
during a quarrel, and dove down a grate,
never returning to find its mate,
who retired to a rear-drawer jumble.
Each lost bauble has a siren wail
that sounds when she's afraid that things won't last.
*Find me! I'm broken! I'm lost!*
What would poking through that cat box have cost?
Giving up instead of leaving
gems of herself behind, and grieving.

# REPAIR

*You have broken yours, haven't you?*
In the dim peeling of years
below the dim ceiling of years
squats a toybox
padded in yellow oilcloth
fresh without a build-up of grime.
Backward in time. . . .
*You have broken yours, haven't you?*

Broken the clock to find the tick,
dissolved the stamp to find the lick,
plucked the lips off a doll,
torn the leg from Sleepy the Fluffy Lamb,
bent the tail of the metal pony,
the sheer examination of what you love,
its destruction:
Texas peeled off the puzzle map,
its statehood
scrolled up like snots.

Breaking
is constructive.
You see how things work
in the moments they are destroyed,
like the prongs of a ring
that once held a birthstone
now not only empty
but . . . withered somehow,
the tiny tines twisted
so the pearl dropped to the stone floor

beneath the pew
where a child dug at her birthstone
which rolled away
and in its absence
she saw its presence made the ring whole.

You might recognize repair as
a square-snouted dog
with one eye.
*At least it has one eye.*
Poor Morgie the dog
—but he can still see
from that felt pad anchored by a button,
damaged but understood.
Damage *is* a kind of understanding:
Look what you've done.
You have broken *yours*, haven't you?

# THE PARSLEY SHIP

When he sailed a parsley leaf toward the storm
out of radio contact, she woke up
in what we'd have to call a love panic
though it's settled that she's not his mistress
(leaflike shadows of that role still mottled
the moving waters of their friendship).
Inside the ship called Friend he ploughed
through a storm as viscous as a dream.
*Did that mean he'd die?* A fear-stab deep
as any penis hoisted her from the waves,
tossing her body up, out of the roil
where he steered his leaf, whose pungent
green whiff woke her with the message
that death is *green,* and she must call him up.

# THE UMBRELLA

The doorman smiles and the esophageal elevator
burps me up to the 21ˢᵗ floor. *You must have flown!*
she says. I close my umbrella.
Then I just have to lie down.


As an April wind blows a pigeon past the 21ˢᵗ floor,
suddenly I say, if only I could get rid of this shame.
*Little girl in Buffalo,* she says.
Imagine the iridescent neck of that pigeon plunging 21 storeys,
but I have 52 storeys to plunge,
what a horrible long drop.
"And now here's Molly Pigeon!" I was once introduced at a
        podium
but I'm *not,* I'm *not,* I'm *something else*
f - a - n - n - e - d
now just a feathered bullet heading into the past.
*It's not ahead of you, you know, the shame,* she says, *is way back there,*
when all I feel is my constant companion,
f - f - f - e - a - r
into the air like a feather.
Tossed into the air by my father.
*You must have been only one or two years old,*
Stop it!!! Can't you see she's afraid? my mother cheeps.
Put me down! I peep.
*but some children love being tossed into the air.*
Late at night, all of six in a panic
pecking along the ledge to the stairs.
All so dark, like an eclipse or a war cloud.
*You were besieged.*
What a relief to hear a word from war

a grief slop bucket of carcassed ugliness:
I have to, I have to, go to the B-
*We have two minutes.*
"Have I got time to go to the bathroom?"
Sinking onto the toilet seat, sobbing and peeing
have to go to the B-, to the Be-
but I'm already *in* the bathroom.
Already there.
The Be- You- Tee- Full Place,
that's what I thought as I closed my eyes, tossed into the air,
I have to go to The Beautiful Place, The Land of the Shí.
Where, where is it?
Blubbering I peck along the hall to the door—
*You can always call me this evening you know*
—and blunder toward my umbrella
my body and my tears and my umbrella slowly
sucked downward peristaltically
where quietly the doors open:

The doorman smiles in the lobby acknowledging my tears,
"It's raining!"
and really it is, so I must open my parapluie
into the blast of slop on 72nd St.
and I do—it is a gift from someone I once showed
how to do something, for saving
what he thought had failed—a peacock umbrella,
iridescent, turquoise, full of eyes, fanned completely out.

# REFUSAL

A fleecy blanket, a furred protection
those balconies of bacteria became
—*my* right by *my* election
transferred to my wild teeth, becoming tame
not through hygiene, but its opposite:
beloved neglect. (Like an unmade bed,
all soft ridges and warrens, or an unknit
sweater in plush unraveling.) "I *said*
I would! Right now!" I yelled from the bathroom sink,
but I could not enter my mouth with the brush
and the false freshness of the paste's tubed stink.
It was homey as leaves beneath a bush
you could crawl under and play house in;
it was my mouthhouse, my inn, and my in.

## TAN OVAL HEAD LEANING TOWARD
## TINY BROWN OVAL SHELL

Little brown bivalve with a ribbon of tissue paper
Glued to its belly,

A solemn little shell.

Now what does it have to clam up about?
Name in one word the task of childhood:  W  A  I  T  I  N  G.

Are you waiting to grow up, little shell?
NO ANSWER.

Solid     Dry     Ridged     Shh—

The shell is a child's toy
Meant to be placed in a tall glass of water.

PLUNK!

Q:  Will you others join me in defining eternity?
A:  Watching the little girl wait for that damn shell to open.

Seepage, then a slit:
White insides.

And a green mass of something
Out of which springs a string,

A magenta paper flower spinning through the water
like a tiny wet jack-in-the-box  -ING!

Participle of a bloom, continu -*ing, ing, ing*
How often does a wait have a reward?

Ask her, Go ahead, ask the girl,
Small mouth composed

In a wavy little line
Like the wavy line of the green thread stem

That holds up the red flower,
Wet,

Not tight-lipped, but close-mouthed,
Her pleasure derived privately.

# LET ME MANAGE SOMETHING SIMPLE
*On Palm Sunday*

Held in the palms of the mass, it's safe
to vanish a moment beneath the red
glass of the rose window, to a bathtub
at the Pierre Hotel for a Roman-style
suicide, blood leaking brightly through
the suds, though I'm right here on a red
folding chair in the Cathedral wondering
why the priests grab the innocent parts while
the congregants have to say, "Kill Him, kill Him!"
I leap up and hurry past the gift shop
to those rickety women's stalls where I vomit.

How embarrassing! I suppose I repaired
to the bathroom of the Cathedral physically,
to do my human act, as mentally
I repaired to the Pierre to kill my young self.
If you and I were introduced here you
wouldn't know my grief had shaped itself into
a gulping girl waving goodbye to her doctor,
flying to Rome for a whole month, the span
of a menses, which the girl awaits so longingly.
Killing her off indeed! How I've needed her energy
to watch each member of my family die.
You may see me as a woman in red earrings,

yet I, two drops of blood at my ears,
have deposited my mind in the care
of a girl in a bathtub (unaware
that one day a corner of this church will burn)
sobbing at her present that's become my past.

Mourning for what was contains
a certain happiness. At least it was.
But it takes more than tears to place your mind
inside your spine, to hear a prayer click
into the music of a spinal chord.
Dear Lord, let that girl climb out of the tub.
Let her take up a practice of words-in-blood.
And let me manage something simple,
like pulling up my socks.
I have had my suffering—and what does it mean?
That I am fortified for what is to come.

# THE LAND OF TEARS

You can stop in the spot you're already in
and enter the Land of Tears. It takes
a liquid thought inside the tin
mixing bowl of the brain pan, full of aches
from the scraping of your mind-spoon to make
the journey of the ingredients, the batter
that you turn out into a pan and bake
back into your old self, now new matter,
all because of that liquid thought mixed up
with your dry milled existence. Curiously
simple tears stop the furiously
churned air, as a door opening up
stops an argument. You know what you meant.
As, after a rain, the air is brilliant.

## COUPLE SHARING A PEACH

It's not the first time
we've bitten into a peach.
But now at the same time
it splits—half for each.
Our "then" is inside its "now,"
its halved pit unfleshed—

*what was* refreshed.
Two happinesses unfold
from one joy, folioed.
In a hotel room
our moment lies
with its ode inside,
a red tinge,
with a hinge.

# DIARY OF OUR DAY IN PAINTING TITLES

Calico Cat?
**COMPOSITION IN BLACK, WHITE, AND ORANGE**

Woman Cantaloupe Coffee Window?
**COMPOSITION IN ORANGE AND BROWN**

Hairy Man Stretched on Bed?
**HIRSUTE FIGURE WITH PERFECT LITTLE FEET**

Yoga ø Back Pain?
**FIGURE IN CAT POSE**

Knight on e-mail?
**UNTITLED**

Slender Woman & Green Salad?
**CELERY CELEBRITY**

It's Your World—Pick What You Want!
**COMPOSITION IN RED ORANGE YELLOW BROWN GREEN**

Little Red Pain?
Don't Go There You'll Never Come Back!
**DISCOLORATION**

Rain Outside a Doctor's Office?
**CLEAN SLATE**

Dental Implants?
**COMPOSITION IN METAL AND ENAMEL I**

Pumpkin Risotto in Black Frying Pan?
**CALICO CAT**

Rejects:
>Peach Bath Oil
>Coconut Macaroons
>Farts
>Kitty Litter

*No titles with smells!*

Maroon Collection?
**MAROONED**

Circle of Love with Clouds and Hirsute Man?

The Nose That Grows After You Die?

Composition in Orange and White
**CRABBY TABBY ON DUVET**

Bus Tires on Wet Pavement Below at 4 AM
*Not a painting !!!!*

**NECESSARY FAILURE OF VISION**

Good Knights (Are Gentle)?
The Parfit Gentle Man?
Woman with Itty Bitty Booklight & Blue Nightgown?
COUPLE UNDER SHEETS PAPERWEIGHTED WITH CATS

*Oh sleepiness*
MIDNIGHT BLUE WITH WHITE CIRCLE FLOATING

# CONVERSATION

A sudden embodiment of our love
dives and surfaces in the water course
of our conversation like a ghost seal,
playfully old, oldly playful,
whiskery but sleek, slipping through what we feel
(our feelings, too, submerged). What makes us full
we hardly know the substance of, though re-
is its first sound: regret, remorse, return,
recourse, resource, relive, revive. We—
now a pronoun applied to us for years—turn
again and dive deep, making water rings
that recircle our love while vanishing.

## THE SOUL HOUSE

To the soul house no guests can be asked
though it is calm as a lake, its shore so prepared
anyone who stops by wants to build there.
But no. Who lives here lives unmasked.
Across the waxed floors slips only a soul
in a soul's bathrobe, tattered of course.
This is what spirits at home wear. That bowl
receives real plums, the vases real flowers.
Soul breath is quite real, too, its naked powers
insisting it be housed exclusively
for its air alone—pure being. And no
secrets in the soul house, only privacy.
A place to grow in, but not outgrow.
Not emptiness, but emptiedness. A source.

# BREAKFAST WITH CATS

The advent of the new habit occurred
the Tuesday the cats ignored us, when I
fell in love with my new electric frother,
overfrothing the milk. Monday *we* ignored *them*.
Deadlines to meet, of course. Never got to make love.
Never eat breakfast at a proper table. . . .
We eat in the living room by the big window
so we can hear every decibel
of the buses' brakes' bellows' breath below
where the East Village spreads out in blocks & streets
like the wheat field squares & apple orchard rows
our cats would roam in—if not for that word "like."

Feeling the deep silence of our cats in their berths
beneath the tablecloth of the table we ignore,
I poured the extra milk in two blue bowls which had
reproached us with their tiny emptinesses
since we had purchased them in Chinatown,
never thinking of a single thing that could go in them
because we had only solid thoughts.
The milk was a liquid thought.
It began to rain on the East Village.
The buses' brakes began to breathe more deeply
as they came to their sensible loud stops,

and by my footstool I placed both bowls.
Delicately the two cats' heads appeared
around the sides of the wing backed chair.
They lowered their triangle chins into their bowls
at the left                          and at the right,
had their fill, circled the carpet medallion,
then lay in the lower ocean of the room,
their habit become a rite in an instant.
And every morning since they each have sat
in the original position of the bowls,
waiting for their froth,
for which gods live.

# FROM *And Live Apart*

## 1 9 8 0

*Surely if each one saw anothers heart,*
*There would be no commerce,*
*No sale or bargain passe: all would disperse,*
*And live apart*

—GEORGE HERBERT
*from* "GIDDINESSE"

# A KIND OF PARLANCE

At 3 PM she feeds the penguins
in her red parka. It is a small marine zoo.

You and I are here. We hardly
know each other, this winter.

Beside her fishpail is the clipboard.
She plunges a hand in the silver mess

then pencils in who seems
to get what fish.

All the gentoo mill around her
except for Rocko, who is sick today.

These penguins do not see
very well out of water.

In the rookery they find
their partners by pitch.

This is somewhere between you
pressing against the screen yelling

Mol-llleee! and the sound of it
whispered in low registers.

But gentoo penguins see underwater
wonderfully, from their camouflage.

To the seal, the black back looks like sea.
To the fish, the white breast looks like ice.

Nor do they swim. The gentoo seem to fly. The water
is sky. The birds are water. The birds are ice.

It is very much like love,
these reversals.

The extremities of warm oils in arctic waters,
the miraculous lids of their eyes. . . .

The woman still called Rocko,
who stayed when the others were fed.

"Are you sick?"
She shifted the pail, straightened her back,

and dangled the last fish.
She called *rockorocko* imitating the gentoo,

a gentle, glottal sound, but somewhat loud,
again, a few times, calling from her teeth.

Rocko came slowly under her arm
at four o'clock in the winter.

She smoothed his head and asked
the questions, "What's the matter?"

"Are you sick?" "What's the matter?"
Just those questions, many times.

Near the marina ice broke against the tugs.
For a moment I felt lifeless,

like the time when I was kept,
for some symptom of my eyes, in a dark room.

I wanted to smoke, or to drink,
or to leave very quickly—then saw

the shoulders of your jacket against the sky
and made the gesture which became a necessity, to look *up*—

and there was no place to go which was right.
So I faced

the fact of our proximity
and the desire I knew

we both felt, to move
slowly under the arm of that woman.

By the rookery, battened for the night,
we both began speaking gentoo.

I whispered *rockorocko* in a low register,
and you asked, in the voice of the woman,

"Are you sick?" so I said, "What's the matter?"
and we echoed the questions gently back and forth,

the two questions, in the midst
of *rockorockos*.

# ANNO DOMINI

It is Palm Sunday, when Jesus rides into Jerusalem,
the brightest picture in the Bible book.

Despite the two dimensions, air
is moving, molecular with spring,

is sweeter, even in this old apartment,
a quintet with Savior and winds.

How porous houses are, to let it in!
If I were directing a comic film of my life,

I'd open with Jesus in Jerusalem,
my mother on the stucco balcony, breaking

off a palm and giving it to me
with instructions to run and wave it

at Jesus. I would take a step and jerk the palm
sideways, and look at her, then up and back,

and look at her, step by step all the way down
until the procession had almost passed,

asking with each spasm of the palm,
Is this right? No, is this right?

# NIGHTWAKE

To startle in the garden and think of you dead,
to veer and find my victim not victimized again,
to fall asleep mouth open and wake
alarmed and muggy soon again—

it is June, that month of fathers and daughters,
when roses are a constant dozen in my married room.
Just what could my father have done then,
that I would want advice from the twelve of you?

I willed him dead at the age of six
and said hello to corpses ever since.

Now to wake from thick dreams of flowers
cut with a family blood,
shift fast in the bed and stiffen,
listen to his breathing to make sure,
want him waking and saying any good thing he knows—

let him sleep.
Face the shut beauties on the bedroom table.
Who needs a dozen silent friends?
It is dangerous to say your good things to them.
It is sentimental to say them to yourself.

Where do you go to say them
when this narrow night refuses them?

Out on Brown Road the body is flat as the black meadow.
If someone came to the side of you now,
they would walk off the edge of the earth.

# WALKING IS ALMOST FALLING

In saying no, you felt as though you lied,
wrecking an old self. But did you wreck it?
Then, from under, the world began to slide.

In fact, you told the truth when you replied.
You took the step and finally saw it fit,
but saying no, you felt as though you lied.

The great snows gone, the galactic glide
begun, the mud-pink gums of earth were lit
by sun, and then the world began to slide.

Its tongue roiled up and curved. You tried
to walk at first—and could, a little bit!
—but stepping so, you felt as though you lied,

for the warm world felt false. It did not hide
its self. Walking on the crust employed your wit:
said yes. Then stepped. (This way the world won't slide.)

But walking on open earth is choice; the tide
of all acceptance is unloosed. Truth, it
is unsteady, the old glum world begins to slide.
You hurt so, saying no, and feel as though you lied.

# THE LAWNS OF JUNE

The lawns of June, flush with the walks and white
driveways of town, grow and are mown. The grid
of lawn after lawn, then drive after drive,
the 90-degree angles of walks, roads
stripped and then tarred flush with the curbs, all these,
smooth, regular as the rules on a fresh
white card pulled from the box of a new game,
or fresh and regular as the game board
itself, the squares prime for our leaping plays,
are what any troubled mind or body
would order: such as, from here to the drug
store is forty-seven lawns, one hundred-
six lawns from here to the veterinary.
It feels good to count in these ways. And smooth,
the sidewalks and streets are very smooth.
An octagonal sign says Stop. Two lines
mean School. The lawns are thick chartreuse gouache,
roads black as silk, straight and fine as surgical
silk, the walks are bandage white. How smooth and
fast the wheels of cars and bikes and skates go,
their yearning unyielding. These geometries
are love's tired proofs: the badinage of wheel
and road and walk and lawn and drive and curb
and sign and line all flush, flushed with a soft
raillery of values laying the grids
we make with one another, a couple
talking in bed, a water glass near
the Bible, a child's torn bear in his arm.

FROM *Raw Heaven*

1984

# THE DISTANCE UP CLOSE

All my life I've had goals to go after, goals
in a molten distance. And just the way snows
in the distance, dense and white among groves
of bare trees, lessen as I approach and show,
not white, but a mix of mud and leaves among rows
of breathing trees, the fantasies that rose
from my young mind, guarded against my foes'
mocking by my own mocking, lessen. I know
what I've approached, and I am very frightened. It shows
in my slipping face in the melting present. Goals
far off are fire and ice, like a walk through snow
toward a blood-orange sunset. But there is no
perfection like that in coming up close, no
purity in intimacy. Embracing the world, nose
to brow with what we've got and lost, hugging old sorrows
as they fade into mud and leaves, is like shedding clothes,
is like lovers saying, *let's-take-off-our-clothes.*
The word is made flesh in their bodies: does is knows.
The world is made flesh by the snows
fading, then merging into mud and leaves, goals
of long ago emerging among trees in rows
in a distance molten as the world comes up close.

# THE LULL

The possum lay on the tracks fully dead.
I'm the kind of person who stops to look.
It was big and white with flies on its head,
a thick healthy hairless tail, and strong, hooked
nails on its raccoonlike feet. It was a full–
grown possum. It was sturdy and adult.
Only its head was smashed. In the lull
that it took to look, you took the time to insult
the corpse, the flies, the world, the fact that we were
traipsing in our dress shoes down the railroad tracks.
"That's disgusting." You said that. Dreams, brains, fur,
and guts: what we are. That's my bargain, the Pax
Peacock, with the world. Look hard, life's soft. Life's cache
is flesh, flesh, and flesh.

# JUST ABOUT ASLEEP TOGETHER

Just about asleep together, tenderness
of monkeylike swells of grooming ourselves
just about stilled, the duet nonetheless
whispers on, unshelving everything shelved
by the day. A head shifted by nude arms
into its right place soothes the crooked habits
of the body. In lips that talk out of harm's
way is a softness known only to rabbits
and sleepers. It shifts them from the almost to
the genuine: a heavy sleep, black and blank,
the void before a dream. At some cost to
this ankle, that hip, one head, one armpit, a shank
slowly curves, a back turns, an ass is fit
to a belly and two bodies lie frankly
foetal, knees drawn, crook into crook, wing by tit
in the orbit of sleeping. And blankly
shifting and waking without waking
is that much touch that is our sleep making.

# OLD ROADSIDE RESORTS

Summer is a chartreuse hell in the mountains,
green after green after green, the wet smell
of possibility in everything. "Doubt him?"
a memory of a friend's voice asks. Yes! "Well,
why do you love a man who's in a tangle
you yourself would never be in?" So I am,
the hypotenuse of a triangle
watching the other two sides in a jam
of history and pain and veils, like veils
of green washing over the mountain spines
on which perch the broken-down summer jails,
pale boxes that housed Chasidim in the pines
years ago. They're richer now, and go elsewhere.
So mice, squirrels, spiders, and raccoons stay there.

The mountains are like the backs of friendly
dinosaurs who, if they heaved in their sleep,
would throw a small car all the way gently
to Syracuse. Moist follicular trees weep
and chatter. I used to be married, goddamn.
Like him, I was in the tangle I'll never be in.
From the third side I had to see the sham,
the last side, the last window to see in.
Inside stolen time and through time's arches
are these places, webbed and dusty now,
mosquitoes humming among the old porches,
overgrown, sloping, askew. They are endowed,
the gnaw-footed dreams of animals' lairs,
with the vacant stateliness of claw-footed chairs.

# THOSE PAPERWEIGHTS WITH SNOW INSIDE

Dad pushed my mother down the cellar stairs.
Gram had me name each plant in her garden.
My father got drunk. Ma went to country fairs.
The pet chameleon we had was warden
of the living-room curtains where us kids
stood waiting for their headlights to turn in.
My mother took me to the library where ids
entered the Land of Faery or slipped in
the houses of the rich. A teacher told me
to brush my teeth. My sister ran away.
My father broke the kitchen table in half.
My mother went to work. Not to carry
all this in the body's frame is not to see
how the heart and arms were formed on its behalf.
I can't put the burden down. It's what formed
the house I became as the glass ball stormed.

# WHERE IS HOME?

Our homes are on our backs and don't forget it.
But we don't stay in them; we think them.
Homes are from our minds. Once I tried to fit,
repairing through remembering, the stem
of a favorite glass back on its head. No loss.
A man in dirty overalls swung down
from his truck grabbing the bag of shards to toss
into the maw of his truck. To me he was a clown
reaching a powdered hand into the garbage bag
and plucking out the glass intact. Thus in my mind
I'd everything I had. And please tag
along home with me now. The paths are blind
with wet new grass behind the rusty gate
where my low blurry child home lies in state.

# OUR ROOM

I tell the children in school sometimes
why I hate alcoholics: my father was one.
"Alcohol" and "disease" I use, and shun
the word "drunk" or even "drinking," since one time
the kids burst out laughing when I told them.
I felt as though they were laughing at me.
I waited for them, wounded, remem-
bering how I imagined they'd howl at me
when I was in grade 5. Acting drunk
is a guaranteed screamer, especially
for boys. I'm quiet when I sort the junk
of my childhood for them, quiet so we
will all be quiet, and they can ask what
questions they have to and tell about what
happened to them, too. The classroom becomes
oddly lonely when we talk about our homes.

# LONELINESS

It shines as broth in a cup meant
to be brought by both hands up to tempt
a waiting mouth under a light shines, low,
somewhat harsh, then flickeringly half lit
as it, itself, is consumed. Slowly the toe
of the drinker curls in a gentle fit
of tension and satisfaction, as in
the reading of a novel's last pages.
Were the wet mouth to speak, it would be
in a voice that hasn't spoken for ages
because the little voice is so far inside
and the way back is a long, ill-lit ride.

# SHE LAYS

She lays each beautifully mooned index finger
in the furrow on the right and on the left
sides of her clitoris and lets them linger
in their swollen cribs until the wish to see the shaft
exposed lets her move her fingers at the same time
to the right and left sides pinning back
the labia in a nest of hair, the pink sack
of folds exposed, the purplish ridge she'll climb,
when she lets one hand re-pin the labia
to free the other to wander with a withheld
purpose as if it were lost in the sands when the Via
To The City appeared suddenly, exposed:
when the whole exhausted mons is finally held
by both hands is when the Via gates are closed,

but they are open now, as open as her
thighs lying open among the arranged pillows.
Secrets have no place in the orchid boat of her
body and old pink brain beneath the willows.
This is self-love, assured, and this is lost time.
This is knowing, knowing, known
since growing, growing, grown;
revelation without astonishment,
understanding what is meant.
This is world-love. This is lost I'm.

# THE SHOULDERS OF WOMEN

The shoulders of women are shallow, narrow,
and thin compared to the shoulders of men,
surprisingly thin, like the young pharaohs
whose shoulders in stick figures are written
on stones, or bony as the short gold wings
of cranes on oriental screens. Lord, how
surprising to embrace the shortened stirrings
of many bones in their sockets above breasts! Now
what I expect, since I've long embraced men,
is the flesh of the shoulder and the cave
of the chest and I get neither—we're so small.
Unwittingly frail and unknowing and brave
like cranes and young kings, the shoulders of women
turn to surprise and surprise me again with all
their gestures of renewal and recall.

# THE LAND OF VEILS

Beth carefully carves the pears into her
plastic bowl while I talk to her mother.
Beth looks directly at our eyes, but we blur
into the foreground, and Beth blurs toward another
land of her own. "You are very grown-up indeed,
slicing that fruit so nicely," I think she'd like
me to think before her mother and I speed
far away through the waters, then land and strike
our tents on the shore of the chest and thighs
of so-and-so's ballet instructor. The talk
of women, the thousand dim kitchens I sighed
in the backgrounds of, hoping just once to stalk
the animals of my mother's friends' desires—
Beth is doing it just right; she does not
commit the sin of commotion; she aspires
toward a grown-up task (fruit salad); she will blot
herself all up until she is a ghost
among the veils and veils and veils of women
laughing in their tents along the coast
of experience, the ripe persimmons
of acknowledged fantasy in their hands,
until the land of her own we believe Beth is in
is among our burnishing lands.

# NORTH OF THE EYES

Sure it's hard to have sympathy with a
healthy pair of arms and legs and hair
growing bountifully and a belly, a
belly on the oversized side, and a pair
of listening blue eyes over a mouth,
a smallish mouth, that is telling you it
can't go on. "I can't go on," it says. South
of the lips, the chin is firm. The eyes are lit
but not about to cry. North of the eyes
a hand with infinite gentleness smooths
the skin across the brow as it removes
the strands of hair that fell into the eyes
which looked so clearly out at the world as
the mouth talked. That gentle hand is part
of the same body. It is hard to impart
sorrow from such clarity, since a face such as
this, wiping its own brow without a hope
of having it soothed, says it has such hope.

# TWO CUPS ON THE TABLE

I can only rearrange furniture
in our tiny fantasized apartment
in Florence, seen through a curious aperture:
the lens of hope, its constant restatement
of every old fact about us.
I remember this and that and try to fit
everything we own in far small rooms, fuss,
muss, shit! I'm lonely, I can't help it!
Out here on my thousand-mile frontier I grow
more barbaric every day! Soon I'll be like
my neighbors. Save me! Can you hear me? No?
We'll lie intertwined till we look alike
through all the nights till we're a hundred and six!

The stamina of my hope: a window open till dusk.

# SQUIRREL DISAPPEARS

From the fence to the fire escape to this
tiny unexpected yard, his manic
tail quick as the fin of a maple seed is,
flip, flip, a squirrel stops for the scenic
view of sky, wires, restaurant rear, and dog.
Then off again. The air's brief clarity,
like an empty open hand before the fog
of belief disperses the disparity
of "here" and "gone," takes a chip out of time,
like a chipped minute out of love when a word,
a hard word, twitches and is off, its crime
the dissolution of where we'd been lured,
the tiny unexpected yard, love. Empty,
then brief bottomless disbelief in plenty.

# THINGS TO DO

Planning and worrying and waking up
in the morning with items on the list
clanking like quarters in the brain's tin cup,
this and that and what you might have missed
or who pissed you off, suspends you in a state
that wishes and hopes for its goal like some
little one wiggling in a chair who can't wait
for when her legs will reach the floor. The numb
knockings of anxiety are like the heels
of sturdy little shoes steadily beating
on upholstery. It's how anyone feels
having been put into a chair, meeting
responsibilities from a padded perch
too big for anyone's ass. As monarchs
we make ourselves small and govern in search
of what we'll grow into. Except we are
as big as we'll ever get and have gone as far.

# SMELL

The smoky smell of menses—Ma always
left the bathroom door open—smote the hall
the way the elephant-house smell dazed
the crowd in the vestibule at the zoo, all
holding their noses yet pushing toward it.
The warm smell of kept blood and the tinny
smell of fresh blood would make any child quit
playing and wander in toward the skinny
feet, bulldog calves, and doe moose flanks planted
on either side of the porcelain bowl
below the blurry mons. The oxblood napkin landed
in the wastecan. The wise eyes of elephants roll
above their flanks, bellies, and rag-tear ears
in a permeable enormity of smell's
majesty and pungency; and benignity. Years
of months roll away what each month tells:
God, what animals we are, huge of haunch,
bloody and wise in the stench of bosk.

# PETTING AND BEING A PET

Dogs, lambs, chickens, women—pets of all nations!
Fur or feathers under the kneading fingers
of those who long to have pets, relations
of softness to fleshiness, how a hand lingers
on a head or on the ear of a head, thus the sound
of petting and being a pet, a sounding horn:
needing met by kneading of bone which is found
through flesh. Have you ever felt forlorn
looking at a cat on someone else's lap, wishing
the cat was you? Look how an animal is passed
from lap to lap in a room, so many wishing
to hold it. We wish to be in the vast
caress, both animal and hand. Like eyes make sense
of seeing, touch makes being make sense.

## WAKING TO THE CHATTER
## OF THE CHILD NEXT DOOR

What interfered was the apartment wall
in the particular place the words tried
to get through. It was too thick. The shortened hall
is like four acoustic mirrors: to hide
sound is almost impossible, and yet
what the child wanted was so muffled
I couldn't discern what it was. Clouds, wet streets,
and a long, long bridge made of waffled steel
which seemed to elongate as I crossed it
toward a beautiful mountain, backlit,
were all elements of the dream in my mind
as I woke. The mountain was a purple
majesty mountain with the Hiroshige kind
of layered snow on top. As the child's warble
of "More!" woke me, I thought, more of what?
then saw the interminable bridge
and realized my neighbor's door had shut.
What I wanted to know in that sudden lurch
of consciousness was *everything more*
so I could answer what the child had asked for
because I'd rubbed its *more* through my dream's edge;
then I knew all this was my childhood search.

# A BED FOR A WOMAN

I sat right up in bed and said, "Help."
I didn't scream it as if I were dreaming
a nightmare. I don't know what I was dreaming.
The "Help" came from a dream core like the pulp
in the core of a tooth. I wasn't frightened,
and that's important since it took all my
energy and self-concern to understand why
I spoke in the darkness but wasn't frightened.
I rose up out of bed like a person
whose fever had broken as this person
had known it would. Desperation,
hysterical shapelessness, was not in the word
as it would have been had I *called,* but I *spoke.*
"Help" was more like an answer. When I woke,
but not immediately, for I was too startled, I smiled
in this bed for a woman, far from the crib of a child.

# AND YOU WERE A BABY GIRL

I loved your smell when you were a baby
high above me lying in your bassinet
amid cotton, flannel, and rubbery
talc. I stood in the mock diaper I'd wet
(a dishtowel pinned around my rear end) and sniffed
upward past the trousered and wool-skirted knees
toward you, taking in a uriney whiff
of the light but deep sweet smell of fleece
that was your infant skin thirty years ago.
When we lie close together now on the beach
on our towels in the wind near the undertow
in a flower of years whorled against the crease
of sand by the tin waves, I catch the tender
spark of the faint comet of your infant
smell, still, and am shocked and won't surrender
and then do—it is all the years have meant,
the damp baby smoke of rivalry unfurled
beyond the salt and oil of the practicing world.

## ISLANDS IN OUR EYES

Islands are magical, like suns and moons,
surrounded by water, as suns and moons
are surrounded by nothingness, black cool space.
Eyes are islands surrounded by face.
Our isolation from the mainland makes
the thoughts inside us circles in lakes
mouthing plummeting stones. The middle
of the widening pupil of the riddle
is what the daily round taught you and me:
how to build a bridge right through the blank sea
and still come out standing, not just somewhere,
but on our island, finding what we want there.

# SO, WHEN I SWIM TO THE SHORE

Living alone is like floating on blue
waters, arms out, legs down, in a wide bay
face to the sun on a brilliant white day,
the buildings of the city all around one,
millions of people doing what is done
in yellow buildings ringing a turquoise bay
in which one floats, in a lazy K
arms out, head back, legs spread beneath the brew
the clouds will make later on. One is
at the center of something of which one is
no more a part.

       So, when I swim to the shore
and go home and lie down, lips blue, cunt cold,
yet clitoris hard and blue and I am still
alone—never again your finger or lip
or knuckle or two fingers or tongue tip—
what do you think I will do? Send you a bill
for my service as a shill in the carney game
you played with your wife? Hell, let's tame
our own monsters. There's this in being out of love:
I own every blue day I'm not a part of.

## CUT FLOWER

From the arms and stems of all the others,
the whole tribe of lilies swaying
as lilies of lilies together, all lovers,
an instinct inside it kept it swaying
away from what looked to me its rooted
place. Its silky orangeness in the vase, alone,
alone and in command of its unrooted
isolated state, was beautiful, for grown
full nakedness right where I could witness it
was beautiful, huge, and proximate.
When I looked at it, I saw my better self
in the makeshift kingdom of a vase. In
cutting it, I cut myself from the swollen field,
out of what I was in, becoming alien.
Thus separation was the power I could wield.

# AFRAID

Hell, I'm afraid I'll be afraid of your voice,
that's why I don't call (and because I'd like
to be grown-up about my phone bill, choice
being a signal of adulthood)! Like
something papery, but stiff, I think
your voice will sound, like the end of a tablet
of paper, no more whiteness or lines set
in sheer availability. My heart will sink
when I see the gray cardboard backing staring
at me, unblinking, the way I think your voice
will stare, if voices stared, gray and uncaring.
I wish you were here. I'd ask your advice
about whether to call. You'd put your arm
around me and we'd talk, our voices warm,
about whether it would do us any harm.

# A FACE REGRESSES

I know that everyone becomes a child
sometimes, but the sunken image a face
becomes, like a small carved pumpkin with a wild
look to its eye in the moment before the trace
of light provided by the birthday candle
in its gut is snuffed out, the face of the child
lined and wizened that is the dry bundle
of wrinkles a grown face takes on, turning mild
everyday living into the knotted mass
of enemy, parent, baby, jealousy, needs,
is horrific in its turning—pass by friends, pass
by labors of years, pass hurt and love—and breeds
the sulphuric smell of snuffed candle and
vegetable rot that is aged desire,
the want to spark a need that, were it fanned
now, would never flame because the air
of the present will not satisfy it and
the air of the past never gratified its end.

## SKY INSIDE

To understand is to stand under the sky
of your own desires. Instincts are always
to grow. Watch that insane boy to see why
he shakes his hands and head and never plays.
He is too busy trying to grow through
the firestorm of terror that shakes him.
People who do not see you will watch you
and tell you what you are according to them,
self-destructive, or tortured, or any
one of the terms the mind employs to put
itself over the matter. The many
nodes of growth on your limbs are unseen; brute
pressure of the sap inside you makes you grow
while the worlds inside you smoke and blow.

# SWEET TIME

The largest bud in creation travels
up the swollen stem of the amaryllis
like a ship in a womb up a river.
When it reaches its height, the bud unravels
so completely slowly that the thrill is
measured, pleasure by pleasure, each shiver
of the petals noted with the naked eye
noting that it is all naked and red
and about to, about to. Something will try
to surface: it is all about surfaces shed,
discovered, it is all about what wells up
in its own sweet time as sinless and sudden
and unfathomed as an old bad word in the cup
of the lips as a private part sits in a hand, unhidden.
Do you know what sin is? Sin is something
pried out before its time, unresolved unreadiness.
There are things that are properly buried
alive—not bones, not treasure—things living
that will emerge and won't be dug for. Their readiness
is making their own sweet ways unburied.

# THE VEIL OF *IF*

Isn't there a word for it? The fine wet
condensation on grapes and plums as if
each fruit were a soft upper lip furred with sweat:
that matte wrapping of moisture erased
with a finger or smeared by a thumb:
that coating, as if the color of the skin
had mixed with whitewash disguising each plum,
each holly of grapes, in the silk of a chaste
wet stocking? Transparency of desire.
Isn't there a word for it?

                  The handkerchief
or camisole of sweat on fruit on a spire
of a limb or a vine. The web ripeness spins.
A tangerine wrenched open, each section
fluttering on the rind like butterfly
wings on a bruised flower, or the erection
of the heads of raspberries: the almost shy
almost cry of Just Before: the drenched skein,
the cloud or web of moisture we rub
away on our way to the fruit. Dub
it protection, anticipation, pain
of If—before the certainties reign.

# MENTAL FRANCE

We adults make love, but I am far away
in a hut at dusk where two lovers lay
swathed in orange light. Near night. A table
across the room, a purple swath of cloth
on the floor (a girl's dress), on the table
two green oranges . . . blur in my thought. Both
of us almost stop moving in the hiatus
that comes while we wait for each other to focus.

What I used to read is real.
The hut was in a book I read for hours
in school, praying to feel what other people feel.
Now that my desires suit my powers
I find a fresh past in this present, cut
from the literature of love like a fresh
wish clipped from a standard prayer: my hut
in France in this apartment of flesh.

## NEXT AFTERNOON

The phlox is having fun, the purple phlox
is having fun, peonies are having fun,
the car is bouncing down the road, a box
of pansies overturns, the fox kit is having fun
catching bugs in the hay in the field
beyond the irises' purple yield
beyond the stream as the muffler warbles
when the car bounces down the bridge. And I
had fun, too. And so did you. Sex is a sort
of racing whitish purple at 3 AM. Why
does love run so far to be near? No retort.
You're not here. The day's fun is a soft but clear
violet violence of were and we're.

# CUTTING TALL GRASS

I love the sound of lawnmowers each year.
There's a woman in her workpants smelling of
gasoline and cut grass, wiping a smear
of grease on her head while blotting a swelling of
sweat from her head under her plastic visor.
I'm not sure whether she loves that machine.
Short grass is none the wiser for the razor,
so the love of mowing it is love of sheen.
But one must love the vehicle, the sun,
the bugs thrown up behind and the swallows
snatching bugs at the wheels to love a lawn,
the old grass spewn in the bleak shadows,
the new grass smelling of wet and slight rot,
to love to live between what is and is not.

# A GARDEN

Whoever loves a garden fears seasons.
This is the highest of civilizations,
a bed in the earth. Great fears are the reasons
for each garden. Simple devastations,
fake death, false dreams, hungers only imagined
—are just the magic of habits compared
to fear of dirt nature, its crouch, the lesioned
back of earth. The swamp's spilled stomach is stared
down by eyes in a garden. Seasons terrify,
they terrify with their strict endurance
and strict abandonment, like parents. Why?
To garden is to love the instance, the dance
of one's reason and the season, a time
seized to be eased: a garden is a rhyme.

# A GESTURE

Something kind done, something kind said
in spite of everything done and said, in spite
of a soreness of mind, is like being led
to a lawn edged with trees in partial light
where a cloth is spread out for a picnic
—or is it a towel? This is not a picture
but, surprised by sun, put together quick,
a meal of invention startled by nature
into being at all—a startled meal,
arrested on a beach towel, drumsticks,
a half-gone liter of wine—a gift of the real,
an imperfect, conscious attempt to fix
something wrong with something kind, beautiful
because the ragged haste of the gesture is full
of half-creation and suddenly wanting
to do something, since something was wanting.

# THE BURNT LAWN

The August lawn is overmown; it's tan,
almost, instead of green. It's dry, not sad.
(It's not going to die.) Millions of bodies ran
through the lawn this summer: dogs, birds,
barefooted kids, and the feet of women
and men, strapped with tan marks from the sun.
The bare calves, fleecy heads, and lemon-
colored buttocks in the distance in the sun
of those two beautiful kids' bodies making
love rolled down the lawn while we watched with drinks
in our hands on the hill one day, taking
our time, taking all the world's time for the links
which would link you and me momentarily.
You noticed them first. I was talking too hurriedly.

# NERVOUS JABBERING

When I lost my watch I thought I'd give up
time altogether. Going around with time
strapped to my wrist was too much to live up
to under the circumstances, and sublime
the circumstances were not: I bolted
my food, clawed into lines, slapped down money,
snapped open papers, walked on blisters, jolted
to halts before elevators, constant runny
nose and sore throat notwithstanding, a saint.
I was a saint when I lost my watch. Prime
life on the hoof. The watch itself was a cheap
little number that literally fell
off my wrist. How was I? Time couldn't tell.
Got to keep, got to keep, not saying what to keep
or who, how, or yet to keep is the talk of time.

# AMONG TALL BUILDINGS

And nothing, not even that girl you love
with the mole on her arm, will be left. Huge
trenches will be dug just beyond the stove
the whole northeast corridor will become
and the dead will be piled in each rude gouge,
even that girl whose left ear always sticks
slightly out beyond her hair. To fix
the names of who died on tape won't be done
since they'll dig quick to prevent disease. Nobody
likes to hear this kind of talk. I always
hated to hear it myself until I began
loving the mortar between blocks, that cruddy
pocked cement holding up buildings so a man
and a woman can embrace in the maze
of what they've built on the errors of their ways.

# AUBADE

The morning is lifted aloft by the praise
and prayers of birds without the noise
of even occasional traffic yet. "Mays"
lift the cloud of "may nots" that were night's voices—
mock, stock, quarrel, sorrow, and snarl. Fine
cries in the skies shout *Tomorrow!* So it is.
Darkness was not a cover. It was shame's time
beat to a rhyme of not/got. "Have" and "save" twist
in the clouds which bear aloft the morning
messages of words talked out loud in dreams
un- or dis- or half-remembered by darning
voices sewing holes that night poked in the seams
through which those words escaped and rose on wings so
to bear the day to what it seems, and sings so.

# BERRIES WHICH ARE BERRIES

A pink plastic bowlful of blackberries—
transported among the enlarged knuckles
of a hand moving past the Marys
and Jesuses on the calendars buckled
to the flowery walls, then dropped on the oilcloth
in front of me, berry juice dripping off
the arthritic knuckles onto the oilcloth,
and berry juice staining the inside walls of
the bowl a blue like ships-far-out-in-the-sea
—as my breakfast. *"Breakfast!"* "Hi, Gram."
Freedom felt as if it swelled beneath me,
sea-like swells of is, are, and am. I am
free today thinking of that moment,
because the thought of our summer routine
frees me as a metronome saves time
by measuring: each thing meaning what it meant.

# THE LITTLE GIRLS

Listening to the voice of an older child
informing a younger child of a "fact"
the kid didn't know, and watching the wild
parental look of the older one and the act
of guarded nonchalance the younger one puts on
changes their colored world into black and white.
The ordinary chrome of days gets wan,
then gray, then just as black as houses at night,
door after door shut, black as forgetting.
The older one's helpless face contorts in
its official meanness, hungry and aggrieved.
The younger face, after the brief bloodletting
(a high-pitched minute of mocking) reports in
for adult ammunition. Both are bereaved.

# THE WEB OF HISTORIES

The sadness that prevails among families
is the web of histories spun, fibrous
and intense and wet, then dried. It multiplies
its strands to the gossamer stickiness
of the web on the handle of an unused
pump in an unlit pumproom used only
in July, when the running waterworks, fused
from temporary drought, don't work. Lonely
spider, catching bugs calmly in the dust,
leaves quick as water dives into the bucket,
leaving you to tear and catch at the web—lust
*is* a sticky mess—all over your arms. "Fuck it!"
and the door slams shut, leaving you dripping
a bucket into the light, swearing and half weeping.

# MY VAST PRESUMPTION

The balloon ride was his birthday present
three years ago. He never cashed the ticket,
I know, because periodically I'm sent
reminders in the mail. "I didn't take it,
not yet," he said for nearly a year. We don't
bring it up any more. I thought I'd try
a rescue, thought I should—the mire he was in,
his father, his job. Since we were kids, a lie
was a sin, still is. He's my favorite cousin.
I'd love to see him way up in the air
billowed over the farms below, the red stripes
teetering from cloud to cloud, from when to where,
far away from bleak here. "I'm not the type,"
he finally said from his own balloon,
never waving, since never leaving home,
the faintly hysterical first good-bye,
"See you again, soon!"

## STUMBLE

Because you've tumbled off what you were on,
for a minute you forget where you're from.
Stumble and bumble. Where will you be
in 2003? What will you see?
Will you have any money? Will you be
where you thought you ought to have been before?
That shit's always at the door. Fate's in the dirt
you dust off your skirt after you fall. It's in
the picayune baby tears your mother, alert
to every change in the weather, rubbed in
your skin, thinking to wipe the tears off. Fate
is overturning: seeing sky instead
of straight ahead. A stumble weans us from the state
of overweening plans, of the leadened, dead
exactitude of schedule. Remember all
the centuries you fall on when you fall.

## NOVEMBERS

Novembers were the months that began with No.
"Oh no." They died in embers. Above were
V's of geese in skies lit from these low
Even fires. The fires of fall were
Mirrors for the feelings I felt before
Being. I'm telling you now I feel I
Exist for the first time! Neither the bareness nor
Roughness demoralize—I realize I
See much clearer what leafless branches show.

# THIS TIME

All the light, all the bare trees, all the clean
windows through which the light through the trees comes,
this is my home. There comes my sister, unseen
through the empty woods, then visible; there comes
my mother slowly through the sunlight; through
the open door my cousin comes, unlacing
his boots. It is as if we are all new
with the newness spring has, a season's spacing
of newness among oldnesses remade,
each "again" made fresh from old "agains." The light
is so full of air, it seems we are made
of air, as the space that is home in our sight
is made of time. Home is the space
so filled with time that time stands still
for it is contained there. Home is where the will
becomes visible. Just as we can see air's face
when it is wind knocking against branches,
time becomes material, and my cousin blanches
at my sister's remark remade from an old
slight, except it is this time, old time controlled.

# DESIRE

It doesn't speak and it isn't schooled,
like a small foetal animal with wettened fur.
It is the blind instinct for life unruled,
visceral frankincense and animal myrrh.
It is what babies bring to kings,
an eyes-shut, ears-shut medicine of the heart
that smells and touches endings and beginnings
without the details of time's experienced *part-*
*fit-into-part-fit-into-part.* Like a paw,
it is blunt; like a pet who knows you
and nudges your knee with its snout—but more raw
and blinder and younger and more divine, too,
than the tamed wild—it's the drive for what is real,
deeper than the brain's detail: the drive to feel.

# WORLD WE SLEEP IN

There's no one to watch us and grin at us
as we scratch each other's asses and smalls
of backs in the blind way of sleep, phallus
breathing in the Y of the thighs, and walls
about us breathing, no one to look down,
like God, enjoying the view in His way,
curling His nostril and lip to frown
at the profane beauty of how we lay
in our bed of beds. The two college kids
who are not our children and who have not
come home for school vacation making bids
for our attention by flinging open—"What?"
"Look at them."—the bedroom door, then stopping,
pleased only as our pleasure reflects on them,
are not watching us. Without God or popping
eyes of sophomores, no one lifts the hem
of our privacy. It is a godless,
childless world we sleep in, relieved that we
are relieved of faith and responsibility,
though that means there's no one to watch us
and therefore bless us. And so I clamber
through my eyes, then fly out from my head
to bless, if I can, our sheeted chamber,
gawking from the ceiling at us in our bed.

# FORSYTHIA BELOW CLOUDS

What chases spring? Almost anything.
Wind chases it into place, of course, every
chance it gets. Pennies in a pocket, jingling
forgotten in a cotton jacket chase it. Shivery
afternoons chasing dusk chase spring. The yawns
of a million people each act as a million
miniature bellows blowing ninety downs
into bloom, and each dawn catches the loose pollen
of spring in its pastel cup. Winter chases
spring into place like an aging annoyed
Angora cuffs its offspring. It erases
anything cozy. Spring is a colder void,
actually, because of its light. Getting
ready, chasing things away by chasing
them into place, involves cold, light erasing.
Spring is a way of embracing forgetting.

# THE BREACH OF *OR*

Broken lines continue, you know, way past
their breaks, as medians in roads do, or
the dot tracings in kids' books, where the last
point is the first point. But it's the breach of *or,*
the breach a break makes when it skids into
nothingness that I'm panicked will undo
me into an enervated void.
That's why I love you; it's how I avoid
the blank *or* between the black lines. That's why
I love my friends. Taking a pencil with
a heavy lead that will leave a line, wide
and black in its wake, connects given lines with
something almost equal to them. Imagine
a little boat trying to connect two
shores with its wake. It's futile. Now look in
the boat at the picnickers, those two
lovers crowded among pears, cantaloupes, fried
squid and fluttering, flaglike, paper napkins—
watch them wipe their lips, open their arms wide,
embracing each other, laughing about their sins.
A pencil made this. Black lines tried
to equal them. The void was a matter of my pride.

FROM *Take Heart*

1989

# HOW I COME TO YOU

Even a rock
has insides.
Smash one and see
how the shock

reveals the rough
dismantled gut
of a thing once dense.
Making the cut

into yourself,
maybe you hoped
for rock solid through.
That hope I hoped,

too. Dashed
on my rocks was my wish
of what I was. Angry,
dense, and mulish,

I smashed myself
and found my heart
a cave, ready to be
lived in. A start,

veined, unmined.
This is how I come to you:
broken,
not what I knew.

# THE VALLEY OF THE MONSTERS

You might think I'm going to tell you where I've been,
but I'm writing about where I haven't been,

as yet. The Valley of the Monsters is a real place
where rocks are formed in monsters' shapes,

as clouds take the shapes people point to in the sky—
only the rocks, of course, are more permanent. To say why

I'm writing audaciously about what I haven't seen
will occupy the rest of ~~my life~~ this poem: the scene

is a kitchen where two dinosaurs, the kind with those little
lizard-y hands and huge haunches, stand in the middle

of the floor guzzling beer and crushing the cans
with their scaly thumb-equivalents. Hah! I *can*

be audacious because I've been here before! I see
it's the Valley of the Monsters of my drunken family!

In fact, I grew up in the Valley of the Monsters, where
minds were formed in monsters' shapes, like what air

currents turn clouds into, shapes in the sky people point at,
feeling lucky to have grasped the fragmentary, but

the minds of the monsters are far more permanent.
The rocks that form the real Valley of the Monsters are meant

to be paid for as a tourist attraction, whereas of course
my dinosaurs with beer cans are a matter of the coarse

substance of unpaid life. The curious thing about expression
is that the simple telling of something begins the motion

of fulfilling the need to say it. Thus it is healthy
to speak, even in rhymes, about where we see

we're going, even if we haven't been there to find
our answer yet. The rocks are quite permanent, I find,

as is the need to expose them to the fantasy
of finding shapes in them, for fantasy is scrutiny.

# BUFFALO

Many times I wait there for my father,
in parking lots of bars or in the bars
themselves, drinking a cherry Coke, Father
joking with a bartender who ignores
him, except to take the orders. I think
of the horrible discipline of bartenders,
and how they must feel to serve, how some shrink
from any conversation to endure
the serving, serving, serving of disease.
I think I would be one of these, eternally
hunched around myself, turning to appease
monosyllabically in the dimness. To flee
enforced darkness in the afternoon
wasn't possible, where was I to go?
Home was too far to walk to, my balloon,
wrinkling in the front seat in the cold, too
awful to go out and play with. Many
times I wait there for Daddy, stupified
with helpless rage. *Looks old for her age,* any
one of the bartenders said. Outside, the wide
endlessly horizontal vista raged
with sun and snow: it was Buffalo, gleaming
below Great Lakes. Behind bar blinds we were caged,
some motes of sunlight cathedrally beaming.

# COMMANDS OF LOVE

The tragedy of a face in pain
is how little you can do for it
because it is so closed. Having lain

outlined in knives, afraid to move,
it cannot move and therefore cannot love.
This is why we say it is a mask,

for the face is so frozen by hurt and fear
it is unable to ask for help.
You can do nothing but stay near.

This is why we hover over those in pain
doing things unasked for and unwanted,
hoping simply with our bodies to cover pain

as if to protect it. Better to go away.
But by asking for help pain is erased,
for the face opens to say what it has to say

and a beauty of concentration overcomes it.
The pain is saying outwardly what it is.
The help it asks for is what overcomes it.

Help me on with this dress.
Get me a glass of water.
Look, I've made a mess.

Both the face of pain and the face of the one
riveted to it in relief believe there's still
something to get, something to be done.

# SAY YOU LOVE ME

What happened earlier I'm not sure of.
Of course he was drunk, but often he was.
His face looked like a ham on a hook above

me—I was pinned to the chair because
he'd hunkered over me with arms like jaws
pried open by the chair arms. "Do you love

me?" he began to sob. "Say you love me!"
I held out. I was probably fifteen.
What had happened? Had my mother—had she

said or done something? Or had he just been
drinking too long after work? "He'll get *mean*,"
my sister hissed, "just *tell* him." I brought my knee

up to kick him, but was too scared. Nothing
could have got the words out of me then. Rage
shut me up, yet "**DO YOU?**" was beginning

to peel, as of live layers of skin, age
from age from age from him until he gazed
through hysteria as a wet baby thing

repeating, "Do you love me? Say you do,"
in baby chokes, only loud, for they came
from a man. There wouldn't be a rescue

from my mother, still at work. The same
choking sobs said, "Love me, love me," and my game
was breaking down because I couldn't do

anything, not escape into my own
refusal, *I won't, I won't,* not fantasize
a kind, rich father, not fill the narrowed zone,

empty except for confusion until the size
of my fear ballooned as I saw his eyes,
blurred, taurean—my sister screamed—unknown,

unknown to me, a voice rose and levelled
off, "I love you," I said. *"Say 'I love you,*
**Dad!'** *"* "I love you, Dad," I whispered, levelled

by defeat into a cardboard image, untrue,
unbending. I was surprised I could move
as I did to get up, but he stayed, burled

onto the chair—my monstrous fear—she screamed,
my sister, "Dad, the phone! Go answer it!"
The phone wasn't ringing, yet he seemed

to move toward it, and I ran. He had a fit—
*"It's not ringing!"*—but I was at the edge of it
as he collapsed into the chair and blamed

both of us at a distance. No, the phone
was not ringing. There was no world out there,
so there we remained, completely alone.

# BLANK PAPER

Blank sheets of paper were my inheritance.
A plain envelope below my uncle's face,
my dead father's life in legal miniature:
the paper nowhere mentioned my name. Erased,

vanishing as the ink had vanished,
I crept from the couch where I slept, TV
still on to morning cartoons, just outlines
of people, as I was, blank inside. To be

was to be denied. I nearly lay my head
on the open oven door, but it was messy
with meat juice and baked-on drips of sauces
I had made when alive. I held me,

rocking my outline below the TV,
where I watched the cartoons from the floor as
I had as a little girl, my father
blacked out on the couch. Now blank paper has

the life I tried to restore there, after
feeling I was nothing. The feeling, too,
is my inheritance, but the true gift
is to re-create all the old anew:

my head on an oven door just repeated
the way I was disinherited. For him to give
me my life long ago was what I needed;
thus what I write both re-blankens my life
and fills it in with a right to live.

# DREAM COME TRUE

The little girl is shy.
She wonders why
on tiptoes, like paws,
there are laws

such as these:
she will never please
however much
she curtsies, never touch

except the dead head
she touches now and
springs away from, knocking
the flowers, ripping her stocking

on the casket that is
so much higher than she is.
She gets nothing
because there is nothing

but pale flowers on a waxed floor,
no more "Stop that!" then no more.
Her father who lies there
will be her nightmare.

# UNEXPECTED FREEDOM

The aftermath of death is a release
to finally grow away from the one
who stunted you. Now you get enough sun.
The aftermath of death is a release
from drunken midnight calls and the unceasing
responsibility without control
of the one who stunted you. You'll feel you stole
this freedom that will in fact come to appease
the unceasing need you have to expand
in the aftermath of death. The release
is the fact that the dead stay dead, thank God, and
you are free now to live until you die,
nourished just by the fact that you're alive
in the aftermath and now you rest in peace.

# PUTTING A BURDEN DOWN

Putting a burden down feels so empty
you almost want to hoist it up again,
for to carry nothing means there is no "me"

almost. Then freedom, like air, creeps in
as into a nearly airtight house, estranging
you and your burden, making a breach to leap in,

changing an airless place into a landscape,
an outdoors so full of air it leaves you breathless,
there's so much to breathe. Now you escape

what you didn't even know had held you.
It's so big, the outside! How will you ever carry it?
No, no, no, you are only meant to live in it.

This wide plain infused with a sunset? Here?
With distant mountains and a glittering sea?
With distant burdens and a glittering "me," here.

## THAT LEAF

That leaf tries very hard to turn over
in very little wind. It lifts a corner
and settles on the ground exhausted, lifts
itself half over but, as the wind shifts,
falls face down eating mud. It hikes half up
in an attitude of prayer, then gives up.
Suddenly it turns fully over, sun
illuminating its dry belly. The sum
of all attempts is change, yet when change comes
it's finally so easy the world becomes
instantly rearranged, present
from past estranged, the old energy spent
in almost angry astonishment.
All the leaf sees is sky, appallingly wide,
though it always was so—depleted, terrified
by sudden perspective, the outside brought inside,
though it always was so.

# BLUE AND HUGE

The ocean's great to look at
because there's enough of it.
It's like music, a substance that

can't be cut up. It has no pit
to stymie a knife. It's like true laughter:
even laugh-o-meters can't measure it.

You can't divide it in half, sure
to subdivide it in tracts.
Like scent, this way it will waft, or

that, diminished, but in fact
not divided. All
in the world can watch: it will wax

and ebb for everyone.
It will crash on the beach, smell
acrid with brine, being for everyone

HUGE. It's blue enough so all can tell
there's blue enough. In this respect it is
not like love, not like a till

full of dollar bills, not like a kiss
or even many kisses, not
like food, like days, like jobs. It is

indivisibly vast and sufficient. What
else is like it? I can't think, for
I am busy dividing: cut, cut.

Poverty says divide, not provide for.
It splits the core.

# THE SPELL

The job in certain lives has been to find **A**
way to live with feeling—for just to **B**
the selves they are requires them to **C**
things they were forbidden to. All the **D**
structive or delicious forces became in**E**
luctable vapors inside the in**F**
able masks of personal traits the wee**G**
boards of their parents created. But their n**H**
ures were disguised, not destroyed.

                                    **I**
have the same job in my life, avoiding the **J-**
hook of Things Not To Say, not to *know* (not ris**K̇**
things, but life-threatening ones, with their deep w**L**
of being unloved and unforgiven). **M**
pathy was my way out. My mother wouldn't ev**N**
feel anything; she actually unlearned how to (th**O**
feeling what everyone else felt was simply **P**
nal servitude).

            Generations got this **Q**
from generations: Don't say what you feel, *you* **R**
*not you*. Generations of liars in a m**S**
one got the next one into became a **T**
leology of undoing. *You are not **U**,*
you must hide what you feel. Behind your **V**
nial mask you must hide, you as a **W**,
as spelling masks meaning, a kind of h**X**
on the alphabet, created to cover **Y**,
not to destroy it, but to make it ha**Z**.

# A HOT DAY IN AGRIGENTO

Temples look like discarded alphabets.
We loved lying in their shadows lazily
deciphering and resting and laying bets

on what they really were for. Easily
caught by fantasy, we no longer cared
why they were there, just *that* they were. Happy

to sit down and drink the water we shared
(having lugged our plastic bottle, and hats,
and camera, through the human dung bared

right there in the sun—where else could you get
relief with no toilets?) we guzzled it down
and splashed it on our arms, hands, legs, and necks.

A girl in dirty, expensive clothes found
us with the bottle and asked us for some.
I said no. As she left, a gagging smell wound

its way out from the bottle's damp lung.
I've often been asked to give what I've saved,
but under the temple I said no, numbed

against the girl, like one of those bridesmaids
who kept her oil in the Bible story
and was safe for the night. I'd hated those maids

until I became one in *my* story,
the shape of the character I'd searched for
surprising me as the temples did: See

how golden but pocked they've become, nor
are they quite decipherable anymore,
at least to those who forget what they're for,

which is worship, the greed of prayer.
"So that's who you are," my friend said. "Thirsty?"
With him I drank, not quite the maid in the story,

but in her shadow, like letters at rest
in new words on a palimpsest.

# THE SURGE

Maybe it is the shyness of the pride
he has when he puts my hand down to feel
the hardness of his cock I hadn't tried

by any conscious gesture to raise,
yet it rose for my soft presence in the bed:
there was nothing I did to earn its praise

but be alive next to it. Maybe it is
the softness of want beneath his delight
at his body going on without his . . .

his will, really, his instructions . . . that
surges inside me as a sort of surrender
to the fact that I am, that I was made, that

there is nothing I need do to please but be.
To do nothing but be, and thus be wanted:
so, this is love. *Look what happened,* he says as he

watches my hand draw out what it did not raise,
purpled in sleep. The surge inside me must
come from inside me, where the world lies,

just as the prick stiffened to amaze us
came from a rising inside him. The blessing
we feel is knowing that *out there* is nothing.
The world inside us has come to praise us.

# PARROTS OF THE WORLD

"Parrots of the World,"
a street-level shop flush with the other
street-level shops in a one-level village
lying like a flag furled

into a long skinny box
(one end at the train station, the other
at an inlet of ocean) was unnoticeable.
We missed it twice, a blue box

on a street of blue shops
tilted toward the turquoise ocean. It's not here,
my love said. It must be, the phone book said so,
I said, noticing the tops

of two macaws' heads
behind a window I'd seen just our own heads
reflected in twice before. (But before we go in,
I've got to tell you, *insteads*

filled my own life
with the blank regularity that these shops
fill their street—many unnoticeable somethings *instead*
of what in my life

I desired.) I desire *this,*
I thought to myself as I looked at my lover
holding the shop door. Under the hanging cages
I gave him a kiss.

He was shyly embarrassed,
and I was pleased. The boy behind the counter
gave me a small parrot to make friends with—
a chartreuse candy kiss

nibbling on my sundress.
Before I buy the bird, I've got to tell you
we'd been lying, one's head on the other's lap
in tanned undress

for hours on the beach.
Our shoulders smelled of salt; our tongues, from kissing,
didn't know whose mouth they belonged in.
All this within reach.

I love to watch you buy things,
my lover said. The bird was scrabbling up his shirt.
It was so tame, it came to both our fingers.
I grinned beneath the wings

of cockatoos, cockatiels,
Amazon parrots, African parrots, finches, toucans, macaws,
and wrote a big check, and learned about the habits
of my new pet. It feels,

I said, No *I* feel happy!
I love to watch you coddle that animal,
my love said, What will you call it? I didn't know.
He said, Call it Happy.

Before I call it Happy,
I should tell you we fell in love so slowly,
past years escarped by *insteads*. What's its name?
the salesman said. I said, Happy.

# FOOD FOR TALK

The bird delights in human food,
claw clamped to the lip of the cup,
and I delight in human good
the way the bird delights in food,
soft and foreign to its beak, wooed
by something not its own abrupt
crack of the seed. So human good
is soft law to the sharp lip's cup.

# JOY

Joy seeps. It's not
the hot sporadic light
that siblings fight
for, or the shot

the deprived demand,
the hot want of Big Love.
It doesn't glove
a feeling hand,

it *is* the feeling
in the hand, like light seeping,
blood transfusing
like light infusing

slow, accreted,
time almost defeated
in its outline,
as lights outline

shadows. Joy goes
at the pace water flows,
a voluptuous sameness
of wave, shameless

because it is not
the end of desire. It does not
cover a cold
corpse of need, or fold

up childhood. Void
of "answer to" or "purpose of,"
joy is the void
that aimless love

diffuses into,
seeking a level, as light
fills up a night
spilling morning into.

# MY GOD, WHY ARE YOU CRYING?

When someone cries, after making love spills
a pail of tears inside, it is the ache
of years, all the early years' emptiness
hollowed into a pail-like form which fills
with feeling now felt aloud, that resounds.

Why would an orgasm make someone weep?
Why, for being loved now when one had not been.
The anger tendered into tears astounds
the lover with fear to have struck so deep.

## MERELY BY WILDERNESS

The breasts enlarge, and a sweet white discharge
coats the vaginal lips. The nipples itch.
A five-week foetus in the uterus,
the larger share of a large soft pear,
soaks quietly there. Should I run directly
and insist that he marry me? Resist
is what we do. It is this: I'm in what
I never thought I'd be caught in,
and it's a strong net, a roomy deluxe net,
the size of civilization. To shun
this little baby—how can I? Maybe
I could go it alone, fix us a home,
never seem to ask why inside the dream
we'd not look beyond, so not ask beyond:
a poor scratch-castle with a beat-in door.
I can't do this alone, yet I am so alone
no one, not even this child inside me, even
the me I was, can feel the wild cold buzz
that presses me into this place, bleakness
that will break me, except I cannot be
broken merely by wilderness, I can only
be lost.

# CHRISEASTER

I woke up to the bleating of a lamb
in the garage-like recovery room
crowded with wheeled beds waiting to be parked. "Am
I?" I asked as I began to disemtomb

myself from the anesthesia, "where I am?"
Why is there a lamb in this garage-like farm?
Something was wrong in the barn. The nervous bleat-cry
continued. When I raised my head in alarm

and saw the green hospital interior
and felt the blood between my legs and was
frightened, I thought, "It is not hygienic to store
a lamb in here!" Of course the bleating I heard was

a baby crying helplessly way down the room.
I had had an abortion and the baby crying
was someone else's, yet mine—the world was a womb
and the room was still a barn. Lying

back in my stupor in the manger, "ChrisEaster,"
I thought, for it was Eastertime, but I had
condensed the birth and death that were
usually separated by seasons as I bled,

then closed my eyes sarcophagally.
Oh yes, the lamb was the Lamb of God, bleating
in hunger and terror in the tomb room, all woolly
and soft with human pain. My heart lay beating

steadily, for I was alive. Marc stood weeping
in the hall, and later watched as I lay sleeping
in the manger, on the bald hill, near the tomb
at home.

# ON THE STREET

A curette has the shape of a grapefruit spoon.
They dilate the cervix, then clean out the womb
with the jagged prow, just like separating
the grapefruit from its skin, although the softening
yellow rind won't bear another fruit and
... and this womb will? Well, this womb *can,*
if two will. Oh, I am sick of will and all
unconscious life! I am sick of the Fall
and the history of human emotion!
Who knows the end of our commotion except
God, the novelist? Once my heart leapt straight
from its socket, say-beating *Change Your Fate,*
yet I found in order to live my heart
had to beat back in its own pocket: the start
of change ending by continuing living
with wet possibility lingering
like a light rain glazing our separate
apartment buildings now where, unpregnant,
unmarried, and with no one to worry over
us in our old age as we were sure this never
born child would, we don our raincoats and goofily
smile under our umbrellas, unceasingly
happy to see each other when we meet,
on the street.

# THE GHOST

The ghost of my pregnancy, a large
amorphous vapor, much larger than me,
comes when I am alarmed to comfort me,
though it, too, alarms me, and I dodge

away saying, "Leave me alone"; and the ghost,
always beneficent, says, "You're a tough one
to do things for." The ghost must have done
this lots, it so completely knows I'm lost

and empty. It returns the fullness and slow
connection to all the world as it is.
When I let it surround me, the embrace is
more mother than baby. How often we don't know

the difference. It's not a dead little thing
without a spinal chord yet, but a spirit of
the parent we all ought to have had, of
possibility. "I was meant to be dead." Thinking

why it said it was *meant* to be dead brings
the tangible comfort: how I used the foetus
shamelessly, how the brief pregnancy showed us,
its father and me, these choices, not shriveling

but choice alive with choice, for as our brief
parenthood dislodged our parents' anchor
and set us anxiously adrift, more
of our lost natures appeared. In my grief,

I never say good-bye to the ghost, for
I've forgotten it's been there. That's what it's for.
The thought of my pregnancy somehow unmoors
the anxiety the choice still harbors.

# THINGS CAN BE NAMED TO DEATH

Things can be named to death,
you know, by talking
about them too much:
as if you were walking

past the same lamppost
again and again
nearly erasing it
by moving past it: ten

times in your trenchcoat
past the diffused light
of the lamp in the rain:
in your mental trenchcoat

the lamppost a feeling
you're merely moving past
while concentrating
on something falsely *else:* last

night, last year, last rain,
the lamppost a real god
behind a false god's name
being named and renamed.

# A SIMPLE PURCHASE

Buying flowers
lowers
panic levels
as bevels
in mirrors
reduce terrors
by taking
images
and breaking
their edges:

freely
buds of peonies
burst from stems
beyond the whims
of the devil.
Flowers are not evil,
though they make belief
in evil easy:
they're so beautiful
that God must be ugly.

They're not in His image,
but what He wants to be.
He sets as His wage
what He wants to see,
for He is cancerous,
crippled,
leprous,
and pulled

toward terror.
God must be error

incarnate!
How else can we account
for evil and still mount
our belief? Hate
must be His state.
Our damage
isn't in God's eye,
but God's *eye.*
It's His image,
the one He creates in,

a state of sin.
Thus the terror around us
surrounds us
because it is God.
Here I thought He was good.
He can barely lift
His scaled hand
to His bulbous forehead
or, for the sores, shift
from side to side.

Not to hide
what He is, but
to gain what
He would be,
He must make beauty,

just as we hope
to change—and grope
toward form in our lives,
even if only the rhymes

of our mistakes survive.
Thus all is pattern.
The continual figure
of a leaf
is the flower
of error and belief
in the world's faults
which are God's faults:
horror
in order.

# HOW I HAD TO ACT

One day I went and bought a fake fur coat
from two old ladies in a discount shop
no young woman should have walked into: taupe

fluff with leopard spots for four hundred bucks
which I charged—no cash till my paycheck—
admired by the two old saleslady crooks.

Five minutes later I was at my shrink's
casually shoving the bag by a chair,
one arm flopping out synthetically. Trinkets,

all belonging to my crooked grandmother,
floated across the wall already filled with the shrink's
trinkets. Afterward, among the minks

on the street, I caught sight of my grandmother
in a shopwindow. The wind was howling.
I wore the fake coat with a babushka. Another

possibility was: that was *me*. I didn't
have four hundred dollars and felt humiliated
by what I had acted out and berated

myself for buying a blazer in the size
*of my sister* the week before! You MESS!
I called myself a lot of names. Eyes

on the bus looked up when I barreled on
in the coat I couldn't return to the store.

I refused to go shopping alone anymore.

My rich friend said, "A fun fur . . . how daring."
How daring to become my clever, lying
grandmother and before that my sister whose loved,

dirty stuffed leopard Gram craftily destroyed.
I had promised myself a real fur coat
which I wanted as I did a real self, employed

with real feelings. Instead I bought a fake
which I couldn't afford. "What a mistake!"
I chortled to my shrink, who agreed

though I did not want her to. How terrible,
I wanted her to say, How terrible
you have to act this way.

## ANGER SWEETENED

What we don't forget is what we don't say.
I mourn the leaps of anger covered
by quizzical looks, grasshoppers covered
by coagulating chocolate. Each word,
like a leggy thing that would have sprung away,
we caught and candified so it would stay
spindly and alarmed, poised in our presence,
dead, but in the shape of its old essence.
We must eat them now. We must eat the words
we should have let go but preserved, thinking
to hide them. They were as small as insects blinking
in our hands, but now they are stiff and shirred
with sweet to twice their size, so what we gagged
will gag us now that we are so enraged.

# FEELING SORRY FOR YOURSELF

Feeling sorry for yourself is the right
thing to do, the moral and human thing,
for it takes you beyond contempt. One night
you may remember an embarrassing
thing you've done (mine, stupidly, was having
a near-affair with my friend's husband when we
were in our twenties) and find yourself masking
what you were with hatred. That word, "stupidly,"
was my remnant of self-hatred. The affair
was never consummated; it was an
elaborately withheld romance. To repair
a self *requires* feeling sorry for it. Can
contempt clarify the way sorrow can?
It's clear to me I was so hungry then,
and I am sorry to have lost the friend
and sorry also that I did not eat.

# THROWING OUT OLD CLOTHES

Throwing out old clothes is painful, because
how do I know I won't need them again?
This one, discolored under the arms, was
worn to dinner—roast duck—with two old friends.
It smells creeky, like floorboards smell; the closet
where it's been jammed smells of bits of stain (duck
à l'orange, crab, pork, veal) dried, pressed, and set
into now-napless cloth. Time to chuck
the lot. What I need again are the friends,
not the clothes, though *they* were friends. One woman
moved back to her hometown and remarried.
That one I sewed, then let fray to the ends.
The deeper friend cast me off for a man.
That friendship—like what to wear when hurried
by one's schedule, the satisfying skirt
one grabs, for it fits and fits till it bags—hurt
not to fix. Ditching loved clothes hurts because
all age does; holes like mouths sag open: *it was.*

# FRIENDSHIP WITH MEN

Is friendship with men like friendship with birds?
Is friendship the way this parrot nestles
beneath my chin, its feathers only disturbed
by the regular wind from my nostrils?

Unexpectedly, another species
and I achieve intimacy: we are
each other's pets; as I imagine the seas
at a great distance are pets of the stars.

# REUNION

Sweat lingering in broadcloth over soap,
the first man's smell I smell belongs to you.
Can't look at myself. I trust you see my taupe
skin on the clammy bedsheets clearer than I do.
The offseason blue snowlight in that broken
down summer motel all college kids freeze in
I see clearer than my own skin. To look in
the mirror you are is the best I can do, woozy
with fear to see what I am. Your chest—I look there—
your mole-y back and neck, scaley kneecaps,
nervous groin. As worried about my hair
as what I'll do in bed, I stick a showercap
on my head the first time we make love
ever in our lives.

How did we stop ourselves
from talking about this? What blasphemy of
our youth we made when we talked of adult selves'
divorces, psychotherapies, and awards—
nineteen years of experienced life behind. Hoards
of things happened to us that don't make any
difference! My dear, I knew you were dying
when you called, and by waiting for you never to tell me
I helped you engage in a form of lying
that stopped the only gift I could give you:
my half of us then, of what we know was true
but must say to be free in it, *I remember you.*

# INSTEAD OF HER OWN

Instead of her own, my grandmother washed my hair.
The porcelain was cold at the back of my neck,
my fragile neck. Altogether it was cold there.

She did it so my hair would smell sweet.
What else is like the moist mouse straw
of a girl's head? Why, the feeling of complete

peace the smell brings to a room whose window
off oily Lake Erie is rimmed with snow.
Knuckles rasping at young temples know,

in the involuntary way a body knows,
that as old is, so young grows. Completion
drives us: substitution is our mission.

Thin little head below thin little head grown old.
Water almost warm in a room almost cold.

# FRIENDS

Friends are our families now. They act
with rivalry and concern, as sisters
and brothers have acted. They repeat the fact
of family without the far-walked blisters
of heredity. Friends echo childhood
but stop childish acts, for they do not require
the child in us to serve. It is our mood
that friends serve and in our mirrors we admire
their faces and ours. Where would I meet
my sister as a friend now? Though I love her,
we have only our childhoods in common.
Friends help me get rid of what we'll never
get rid of: our terror of the childhood we shun.
How sick I am of it! Yet I am it, which
my friends know, for they feel it as we embrace,
as I feel their families coursing through them. We itch
to understand what we cannot erase
but can no longer live inside of. Thus
we confide in those outside we bring beside us.

# THE WORM

"There's a worm at the bottom of each bottle!"
you cried gleefully at the faculty table
I'd commandeered for my friends, having startled

the whole room by worming that table
for my student, husband and unstable,
grimy, nonfaculty confrères. *I could throttle*

*my own sister,* I thought as I looked at you,
a tawny albatross, eyes bright, hair wild.
Now all your rotten stories would ensue,

and I'd get nervous, me the useful, mild
young woman on the college support staff, a child
to be doing such a job, though I had raised you,

and there you were, a baby whore, regaling
my modest friends with life in Mexico,
mescal! peyote! "What's wrong with a little fling

just for the money?" you exclaimed. *Just go,*
I thought, *just leave.* But how can a burnt rose
unfurl its lips and just leave the garden? "String

the older ones along. The pay's higher!"
I'd done a terrible job on you, so of course
I took you in again. *How could you be what you are,*

I thought stonily. What beauty your coarse
words had and how beautifully your long, coarse
hair swung against your shoulders, fresh fire

in blonde toss. ". . . an ugly little beige worm
at the bottom of every bottle! I mean,
how does that worm get *in* there??" That was the warm

pebbly tone of your whiskey voice at nineteen.
I was twenty-two and dead then, slain by the fiend
of motherhood and sisterhood, the earth infirm
about my turning corpse, riddled by the worm.

# I MUST HAVE LEARNED THIS SOMEWHERE

I loved an old doll made of bleached
wooden beads strung into a stick figure.
When the string was pulled, the tautened limbs
reached their full extent, and a human figure,
stiff with rigor mortis, rose up.
When the string was let go, the doll collapsed
into a heap more lifelike, though it missed
its spinal chord of string. I spent hours trying
to prop it up to look more human without
pulling the string, but it sat in my hands,
bent, uncontrolled in a muscular fit
or a spasm of fear. And so for myself,
collapsed in a tangled necklace,
anger painting my stiff wooden face.
Yet now my life can hold me in its hands
as long ago I coaxed the doll in my palms
to try to sit lifelike there. My mother's hands
must long ago have offered the same balm
though I took her for an operator
holding my string. How else could I store
such an idea of comfort as I
gave the doll, so material was its cry?

# ART BUZZARDS

*at the Albright Knox Art Gallery,*
*Buffalo, New York*

Nude mental life was what fed me: Arp's brass
star, a Giacometti, Jackson Pollock's scrambled
anger, the ugly yellow Christ I passed
on the way to the café where I mumbled
"cream cheese on raisin" and sat near the frozen
window. Outside were sculptures in the snow.
I was frightened by the walls' white horizon
and the braceletted women, though now I know
they were only art buzzards, as I was to be.
From high school this nude mental life took three
busses to get to. The art itself was free
as I was in the café, suffering
the arty taste of the ice cream: clove.
What began there was a kind of love, clove
of art and love of self.

                Government sponsoring
of cheese giveaways for senior citizens
brings my mother and me here on our jaunt.
It only half surprises me that she'd want
—after standing in line for cheese in a high school—
to distract herself with thought. "Vicarrions"
were what I called art buzzards in high school.
I am so pleased to find my mother is one,
or pleased I'm able to notice at last. "That one,"
she says, "it's a beauty." Max Ernst. Then the pool
of the blue eyes of teenage *Lady H,*
next to a painting of Shakespeare's cottage.
From room to room and thus through centuries

we go, often in agreement, our taste
given a distracted history, classed
along with similar hands, feet, bodies
of nude knowledge as well as naked
bodies in common.
                        Picture how we are fed:
enormous birds over frozen terrain
strewn with the offal of those dead to pain,
we land and are glad of nourishment of heart.
From our beaks hang the gizzards of art.

# GOOD GIRL

Hold up the universe, good girl. Hold up
the tent that is the sky of your world at which
you are the narrow center pole, good girl. Rup-
ture is the enemy. Keep all whole. The itch
to be yourself, plump and bending, below a sky
unending, held up by God forever
is denied by you as Central Control. Sever
yourself, poor false Atlas, poor "Atlesse," lie
recumbent below the sky. Nothing falls down,
except you, luscious and limited on the ground.
Holding everything up, always on your own,
creates a loneliness so profound
you are nothing but a column, good girl,
a temple ruin against a sky held up
by forces beyond you. Let yourself curl
up: a fleshy foetal figure cupped
about its own vibrant soul. You are
the universe about its pole. God's not far.

## DON'T THINK GOVERNMENTS
## END THE WORLD

Don't think governments end the world. The blast,
the burnings, and the final famine will
be brought on *by mistake*. "I'm sorry," the last
anxious man at the control panel will
try to say, his face streaked with panic, red
hives rising on his neck. He'll have been a jerk
all his life, who couldn't get through his head
that his mother couldn't love him. Work
at the panel would give him the control
that she had denied him again and again.

Thus the world will burn through the central hole
of his being. He won't really be sure—again,
having never been assured of her—of what
he is supposed to do. That is, he'll be sure
at every exercise until the shut
blank door of the final moment injures
his jerry-built control and **BANG, BANG, BANG.**

It won't be his fault, his childish mother's fault,
or the fault of what produced her or what
produced what produced her back through the vault
of savage centuries. If he'd just known what,
he'd have done it to please. He might have known himself
through what he'd felt, and thus might be clear.
She might have said, "That's nice, dear,"
and we wouldn't be dead.

Aren't you scared of your life in his hands?
But of all the men whose hands you'd hope to be in,
Name the one you're sure of. The history of nations
is cold; the world burns by generations.

# CHOICE

To become conscious of all around us
or to live in watery, unconscious worlds
is the only choice guaranteed us
by creation. Punishments of words,
enslavement, beatings, illnesses, debt, and all
else that murder a self do not murder
our choice: which is *to know, to feel,* or fall
down the endless dreamlike tunnel in world-blur.
The pain is just the same either way.
Choice makes nothing go away.
To know just what we're born to is all
we know of why we live and to deny
our choice will kill what freedom we might feel.

# WHEN I LOVE YOU

When I get on the plane, alone again
after being pressed and pulled, and lean my head
against the window until someone bangs
a briefcase into the next seat, your hands
sometimes come to rest on my cheek and head,
turning my real face toward invisible you
waiting in New York, hands flatly tender
as the wingtips of an angel's hands—you
*are* an angel momentarily, treating
my wound of love. Then I feel, to a depth rendered
painful in my exhaustion, a retreating
into a love of your love that moves me
as the plane gathers itself,

                              but the bulk
of someone next to me removes your hands
for I am required to shift. As, invisibly,
they disappear, I am left with the fully adult
knowledge of my vacant self in your absence
and sit alert, but overpowered by the span
of distance between us, and by all spans:
that of your hands and that of our lives.
When I love you with a feeling of breaking
apart as the plane breaks from earth,
all is in fragments: the wingspan
of the plane bursts the angel's wingspan
which regathers as the span of love's aching
across the world's girth.

## ONE PLACE

To live in one place always, like a front
of weather that hovers always above
a coast, your hopes and ideas lighting
the air over the land's head you love,
is like being in love

over years and years, the sums
of accounts and bristles of genital hairs
known and re-known, till the land
is reknowned for the depths of light embossed
so deep their source seems lost.

# ALTRUISM

What if we got outside ourselves and there
really was an outside out there, not just
our insides turned inside out? What if there
really were a you beyond me, not just
the waves off my own fire, like those waves off
the backyard grill you can see the next yard through,
though not well—just enough to know that off
to the right belongs to someone else, not you.
What if, when we said *I love you,* there were
a you to love as there is a yard beyond
to walk past the grill and get to? To endure
the endless walk through the self, knowing through a bond
that has no basis (for ourselves are all we know)
is altruism: not giving, but coming to know
someone is there through the wavy vision
of the self's heat, love become a decision.

# DEAR HEART

Heart, unlock yourself. Fibrillating wings,
undo your ungolding. Impoverished
by the guanoed bars' tarnish, your age sings
battened in a cage. Is that what you wished
when you planned, plotted, picked, posed, and proposed
a life you imagined for yourself, a life
*designed?* Yet you leave your lock unsigned. Closed,
the lock's frozen dry by worry. A knife,
please. Disiridescenced heart, scrape the rust,
oxidized hysteria, from the baroque lock,
for bindings are always baroque, their trust
placed in outwitting. Security mocks
what it locks up to save. See the poor heart,
ashamed at its depletion, angel-bird
picking at soiled feathers, pulling apart
what it meant to preserve while the world occurred.

# THE SMELL OF A GOD

Taking someone inside yourself (like a god,
cinnamon-colored and smooth, sitting on
a tiny platform in your soul) is a process of love,
and the surest method of change. All gone
are the bumpy exteriors; essence is within
essence. The person is not a god
to be worshiped, but one alive within,
an ignorably present household god
whose being permeates your soulroom, its image
so internalized it becomes vaporized—
as an alcove, emptied, is permanently hung
with an odor of cinnamon only recognized
when its essence is present on your tongue,
as in saying something the person might say.
Genelike in soul, you two are related
so thoroughly that even when you pray
(if the real person becomes lost to you) belated
prayers for the person's presence, or even
the presence of the idol you first took in,
you are a haven of scented likeness.
And with its own peculiar nod
smilingly askew
you conjure up your god.

# TRYING TO EVANGELIZE A CUT FLOWER

Poor rose, you live a coda in a glass
coffin on a desk above the Last Will
and Testament of the desk owner. As
you are at the end of your life I will
invite you to join my religion: Church
of Limits. Join me in my gladness not
that things will end, but that we'll end the search.
The pleasure in knowing what you've got
is the love of you, and you are god. Is rage
still your prayer? No, this isn't Church of Cold
Comfort, it's your Church of Rose Comfort: walls, age,
borders, vases, all boundaries that hold
one say, "See what you've got and what you're not."
The Last Will defends its choice to the ends.
Mastery's possible within the limits
of faith in death and the practice of dearth,
little rose, life up close when the gates have closed,
Church of Limits, Church of Worth.

## DEAR ARM

The only thing that's whole is our effort
to remain so. Oh arm, stop your bleeding.
Coagulated stump, deficient, embarrassing,
courting a lost hand which no longer retorts
to your blackened lip of blood, the test of faith
is a nice test to pass, and you can pass it.
It requires no manipulation, and it
demands imperfection. Unswathed, unlaced,
you enter the Land of Unwhole, a large
calmly busy place approached through wide
expanses. Here exteriors are beside
the point, for the interiors are in charge.
Your inabilities bespeak themselves
because they are what you show, wholly.
You have no hand. You cannot help be holy,
for handicapping is complete—no halves.
The test of faith is passed by being whole.
Our compensating efforts leave us full.

# THERE MUST BE

There must be room in love for hate.
Allowing love to behave like a lung
allows hate in—and out. But the state

of nakedness this natural act requires,
have we the natural strength for it?
Or do we, after all our building, tire

of breathing because we are breathing so hard?
Having worked so long. Having built and rebuilt.
The four lungs in this house breathe with regard

to the continuance of our lives
and have the power to squall out the memory
of their earliest squallings, protests that survive

building and meaning. They can take love in
and breathe hate out and so manufacture
another part of the structure we determine

to live in. There must be room enough
for hate, for many rooms will be constructed
from its labor. Presume that love has room

for all other emotions, and resume, resume.

FROM *Original Love*

1995

*First Love*

# THE WHEEL

Because of your nose, like a leaf blade
turned outward; because of the veins, also
leaflike, but stronger, surging up your forearms;
because of the moles spotting your arms
and neck and face like a long mottled animal;
because of the thrillingly perfect grades you made;
because no other girl had you (and I felt
you might want to be had) and beyond this felt
you would not refuse me, I made my play
at Junior Carnival, and threw myself at you
as if I'd done it a thousand times before
(and of course I had—I'd thrown myself away
demanding my parents' love), as if I knew
for certain you'd receive me at the door

of the side gymnasium, flattered, shy,
talking quickly back to me, leaning your shoulder
against the threshold, me leaning closer,
smelling your laundered shirt, you not questioning why
I had chosen you, the one gripping the math folder,
gently accepting my self-exposure
(so needing acceptance yourself); because
of all this I ask you twenty-five years later
to be my husband and you ask me
to be your wife, our first wishes
confirmed at last as our best, spun out, original,
as if our lives were a novel ending (it really
makes sense you left math for literature) with kisses,
and from the games in the dim gymnasium, applause
as our frozen wheel of fortune thaws.

# SO WHAT IF I AM IN LOVE

The penguin sweatshirt I slept in smelled both
of him and time, if time has odor, worn,
softened as skin asleep, blurred as the breath

beneath the faded lines of a bird born
on a shirt, not in a nest. Completely torn
between delight and the imagined wrath,

the sheer disaster of my life torn down if
the shirt were ever found, I accepted
his gift and got on the subway with

my makeup, my papers, my underwear
all stuffed in the bag where it lay, given,
given to me! in my lap in the glare

of trainlight. "Beware," the panic-driven
self says, "No, no you can't," even
at the cost of your growth. But I left it there.

When the doors opened, I leapt out, turned around,
saw it on the seat as the train rushed past,
screaming "No!" so loud a man turned around.

"I left a gift on the train," I said, aghast.
"At least it wasn't cash," he said while the past,
worn, softened, blurred as the lines of the bird,

a comic little figure in the arctic waste
of the white shirt, unfroze inside me, stirred
by the loss and relieved by what I dared

at last to feel. I wobbled home as if
tossed from floe to floe of a broken jam,
from if, to am, to so what if I am.

# MY COLLEGE SEX GROUP

All my girlfriends were talking about sex
and the vibrators they ordered from Eve's
Garden which came with genital portraits
of twelve different girls. All my friends' needs
swirled around me while their conversations
about positions crescendoed and they waved
their vibrators—black rubber things. Saved
by volubility I looked at the relations
of labia to clitori—look, there was one
like mine, labia like chicken wattles
below a hooded clitoris. "Friends!
of these twelve genital portraits, which
are you?" I couldn't ask them. Happy
to have found a picture of one like me:
the portrait held the hair all back and popped
the clitoris out like a snapdragon
above the dark vaginal stem.
Oh God, it was me! (And another, I stopped,
there were others like us, throughout the world.)
When my order for the vibrator was filled,
I'd get my own portrait. I'd show it to the next boy
before I got undressed: "Here's what you're getting."
*And I'm not alone, or ugly, if that's what you're thinking.*

# HAVE YOU EVER FAKED AN ORGASM?

When you get nervous, it's so hard not to.
When you're expected to come in something
other than your ordinary way, to
take pleasure in the new way, lost, not knowing

how to drive it back to sureness . . . *where are*
*the thousand thousand flowers I always pass,*
*the violet flannel, then the sharpness?*
You can't, you can't . . . extinguish the star

in a burst. It goes on glowing. That head
between your legs so long. Could it really
want to be there? One whimpers as though . . .
then gets mad. One could smash the other's valiant head.

*"You didn't come, did you?"* Naturally, he knows.
Although I try to lie, the truth escapes me
almost like an orgasm itself. Then the "No"
that should crack a world, but doesn't, slips free.

# PANTIES AND THE BUDDHA

Frantic to finish, frantic not to forget
details for a thousand deadlines,
"Clean underpants!" I think in the shower,
get out, drag a plastic tub, and string a line
under the tropic showerhead, grabbing clothespins,
hauling soap and dirty silk panties back
behind the curtain with me, still wed
to ALL THINGS NOW! (Poor Buddha, there's an ax
in your back.) *Make of yourself a lightness,*
Buddha says. Loofahs, gels, rinses, and shampoos:
timing the hair rinse to rinsing the pants
—clip each by its crotch, lace dripping.

I won't know I have a body until you,
darling, imagine this lingerie on me as I
excuse myself to the ladies' room stall
of this restaurant in a foreign city
to lean my forehead on the marble, all
items on my lists crossed out, and the ax
I put in the Buddha's back starts slipping out
as I hike up a silk jungle print on my ass,
glad to remember I have one, as you
always remind me how glad you are to feel
this silk beneath the plain wool of my slacks.

# THE RETURN

When she opens her legs to let him seek,
seek inside her, seeking more, she thinks
"What are you looking for?" and feels it will
be hid from her, whatever it is, still
or rapidly moving beyond her frequency.
Then she declares him a mystery
and stops herself from moving and holds still
until he can find his orgasm. Peak
is partly what he looks for, and the brink
he loves to come to and return to must
be part of it, too, thrust, build, the trust
that brings her, surprised, to a brink of her own. . . .
She must be blind to something of her own
he'll recognize and look for. A diamond
speaks in a way through its beams, though it's dumb
to the brilliance it reflects. A gem at the back
of the cave must tell him, "Yes, you can go back."

## LOVE WALL

Because you know you are not me and
I know I am not you, I love you and
am content among my pillows, prints, and
flowers in my room next to your room. The bond
of love that binds our days without a magic wand
to blur the boundaries between my soft land
and your crisp room's equipment, awards, and
lean black frames removes the command
to merge, merge, and die. My mother's hand
snakes around the banister and gropes. I shut
the door. *But you are me,* it cries, *I am you, cut
off from your own wrist!* Quick I look down: two hands,
—both mine, at my arms' ends—proof the command
is disobeyed. I think of leashing her hand
to keep it as a pet, but leave my door shut,
as if telling my neighbor's cat to go home. And
you who are not me work in your room, blandly
remaining separate, our wall our ampersand.

# WAKING UP

I try to keep the promises I make
—for each one broken breaks the world—and seem
inhuman: no crack, no fissure, no mistake.

Control of life is fear for fear's own sake.
A teacup soldered or a split of silk reseamed:
fixing them, I keep the promises I make.

To lower the pressure, I lower the stakes;
the weight of covenants can make me scream
inhuman howls at my human mistakes,

a perfectionist caught in an earthquake.
I lower the stakes and whimper in my dreams
a prayer for a whole life (a promise *kept*) to make

sense. How childish I feel when I remake
childhood's dream: all things delivered in a stream
of consistency—no crack, no fissure, no mistake,

all done when planned. But swans arrive at their lake
each year, called home by the angle of sunbeams.
Surrender to nature's perfection means

to know one's nature, no mistake. Sometimes it seems
a life's asleep beneath my frenzy, and I wake
from a promise of youth that I no longer make.

# THE SCARE

When the nervous excitement in his voice
spreads through the phone like watercolor on
a wet page and first I brighten, then hoist
myself up in bed and turn the light on,
unaccountably asking him what's wrong
(is something offcolor in his brilliance?)
he says that he lifted something up wrong,
felt a pull behind his rib, poked in the dense
tissue beneath it, thinking he found a lump
not quite like the lump from his last cancer,
then he really knew, it could just be a bump
from the weight strain, this anxiety recurs
whenever . . . "Of course it recurs, you idiot,
we've just gotten married!" I don't say.

Images of helping him die spill, like aquatint,
across the sheets. "Not now," I don't pray,
and the dry sheets of my bed feel wet with
the painted images of the hospital bed,
the drip of the IV, radiation, chemotherapy,
the cancer spread, the bedspread wet with
—I've upset a glass of water. "Now listen
I love you, please get on the plane, your rib
will heal, then we'll feel for the lump." Glisten
of adrenalized halo . . . A shining nib,
my voice draws counterlines on his bright fast
voice strokes. How will I ever keep it up?
Don't crawl into prayer posture yet. *Hang up.*
*Shut down. Dry off.* You've got to last.

# MARATHON SONG

I love you at the finish line.
I love you wishing you had run.
I love you saying you will next time.
I love you at the marathon.

We stand here on a big flat rock
on which we've placed a big fat book
so we can get a good high look
at all the runners near the clock.

I love you in repressed fear,
expressed hope, panic, fervor,
and hypocritical nonchalance here,
where heels grind up the past and future.

I love it that only a minor
injury kept you from the up-stepped
training a long-term cancer survivor
must do—now you're all prepped

to run for your life again next year.
I love you in mortal fear
and when the center goes dark.
I love you on a book in Central Park.

# THE PURR

As you stand still in the hall thinking what
to do next and I approach you from behind,
I think behind must be best: your naked
rump scallopped beneath the plumb

line of your spine's furred tree. But
as I catch the concentration in the kind
angling of your head toward the cats and tread
catlike myself behind you, your scrotum

hung like an oriole's nest, I cut
beneath your outstretched arm and find
I'm hungry for your face instead,
hungry for our future. The mysterious thrum

that science can't yet explain awakes a hum
in me, the sound something numb come alive makes.

# LULLABY

Big as a down duvet the night
pulls the close Ontario sky
over the naked earth. Here we lie
gossiping in a circle of light

under our own big comforter,
buried nude as bulbs. I slide south
to grow your hyacinth in my mouth.
Far above, the constellations blur

on the comforter that real sky
is to real earth. Stars make a pattern
above; down here our pattern is fireflies
on flannel around us. Night turns

to surround the planet. Earth settles
real hyacinths in place. You yield,
turning like night's face to settle
on me, chest on breasts, your field.

## BLUSH BLESSING

Luxury is in the ordinary. When
I step into the crowd, I see they grin
at the bus driver and drop in the exact
change they've had time to remember. They're not in
trouble, it seems, or in chemo, in X ray, in pain; in fact
it seems they're in their own heads, not worrying
whether they or those they love will die or why
things are the way they are. I join their ring,
pearled; their world, adored; and cry their cry
of mild annoyance at the tiny imperfections
we all have time to notice. This attractive
woman on the bus for instance, in a red concoction
of cape and boots below her black hair—just to *live*
to note this final, off detail!—has put

*pink*, the wrong color for her outfit, on her lips.
How imperfect, her slightly misshaded choice.
(What's required is a creamy carmine red
the color of her cape.) Darling, when this bus
delivers me home to our clean apartment to be fed
the meal over which I had the time to fuss,
let me make a little fuss about something
insignificant, the malfunction of some silly
piece of hardware, or the wrong hair coloring,
or details for our party, before we pile willy-
nilly into bed with chocolate and video and prepare
to make love. The way a radiator hiss
makes a perfect indoor snowy silence hush,
the flicker of a bother trues the world in which we kiss.

## LITTLE MIRACLE

No use getting hysterical.
The important part is: we're here.
Our lives are a little miracle.

My hummingbird-hearted schedule
beats its shiny frenzy, day into year.
No use getting hysterical—

it's always like that. The oracle
a human voice could be is shrunk by fear.
Our lives are a little miracle

—we must remind ourselves—whimsical,
and lyrical, large and slow and clear.
(So no use getting hysterical!)

All words other than *I love you* are clerical,
dispensable, and replaceable, my dear.
Our inner lives are a miracle.

They beat their essence in the coracle
our ribs provide, the watertight boat we steer
through others' acid, hysterical
demands. Ours is the miracle: *we're here.*

*Mother Love*

# THE SPIDER HEART

Sleeping with my husband in my mother's bed
the night she died, I expected the tree—
the one that Emerson said grew tall and wide
after his father died—but woke up instead
with a spider wedged in my ribcage, scrambling.
It was crablike, black, and horizontal,
like a squat tree on its side. One set of legs
was the roots thrashing against my ribs; the other
was short energetic branches without leaves.
It was a stunted winter tree. It was a winter night.
I lay cold and frightened under my mother's quilt,
but I covered up my husband instead,
lying there, a bit corpselike from exhaustion,
but breathing, while she was being driven
to her hometown, where her plot was.

Death opens the plot of a life: all during
the hideous book of her illness I thought
she had a sad, terrible life, but in her bed
the spider's clawing grew so sharp I had
to count to calm myself down, and so I gave
each year of her life a number, expecting
bad after bad year, but adding up the worst
at ten, a seventh of her life—no worse
than anyone's! Why had I misjudged the pain?
The same ten years quartered my life, doubling
the dose of her daily absences, the helpless
fights with her husband when she returned,
and my constant, childish fear we would all die
from her going away. Then I knew

the terrible scrambling was my own survival.
And I slept, despite the racket in my ribcage,
startling to the alarm on my husband's watch,
heart pounding from waking without enough sleep.

It was time to get going, but I lay there.
I wasn't going to have Ralph Waldo
Emerson's tree. The huge arachnid lay there.
I decided to describe it to my husband
to make it smaller; then I could get up
and we could drive out to my mother's town.
And so we looked hard behind my ribs
and the spider changed under our watching eye,
its thorax elongating, its legs flexing
ballerinalike, its color fading
to the translucency of dancer's tights, silvery
as birchbark—one set of legs rootlike,
whiter, one set branchlike, darker, though still
horizontal. As we got out of bed
I had two limbs of a thought at once:
*You haven't seen the end of that spider*
came first; then the other,
*How will you set the birchtree upright?*

# SEEING A BASKET OF LOBELIA
## THE COLOR OF A BATHROBE

*in the galley of a barge*

At that time I read a book about a girl prone
to perfection: her mother had just died.
As she prepared her first supper, she tried
to peel each potato so that not one eye
remained—a perfection of paring. And I,
who also often prepared supper for
my father in my mother's absence, power-
fully attached myself to that girl's unsparing
idea of the world, brooking no mistakes, daring
those still alive to rise to her new standard.
But I couldn't come up to it, lured
though I was by the thought that my goodness
would prevent all evil, even the drunken mess
our family was in. Instead of crying out,
I accepted a tranquilizer, whirled
in a bath of remorse, then curled

in mother's bathrobe, blinking my potato eye
through the haze of a drug she gave me
—my father's Librium—at a loss for what
else to do, since I wept uncontrollably,
begging her to leave my father and save
all our lives, though there we all stayed.
Now baskets of perfect lobelia fly by,
each flower bathrobe blue, with one white eye.
I peel potatoes below, looking out the little
galley window at their blue, untranquilized,
having left that house so long ago. *Now Dear Miss,*
*you wanted perfection . . .* and found it, whittled

down to a book I couldn't obey. *Be good,*
but leave each potato her imperfect eye,
because something must be left to cry
the tears stored in roots brought out for food.

# THE RULE

Completely naked, mons completely gray,
my mother tells me how to masturbate
leaning over the couch where down I lay
in my dream. But I know how! You're too late!
Too often we have to wait for our guides.
Completely naked, mons completely brown,
will I invite her to lie down, who prides
herself on never touching, let alone
holding, stroking, licking? I don't,
though if I wait perhaps she will come of
her own powers, and then we will make love.
Will we be guilty, taking our love loaned
from a dream? Or will curiosity
free us from "Be Still," and let us be?

# THE JOB

Seized by fear and anger at my first job
—everybody told me to blow off steam—
I got migraines on weekends, made to rob me
of what everyone called "my fun." Prone, in dream,
drugged by Fiorinal in a darkened room,
I had a kind of respite. When the pain
stretched my skull into a filled balloon,
I fantasized a pink rubber topknot,
a sphincterlike valve to release the blame,
the terror and panic—the steam. I forgot
all about the sphincter, though I'd felt then
it was God's mistake to make us without it,
until I saw a nurse remove a bandage
from what was my mother's clear field of skin
and saw the sphincter reinvented again
as metastasized cancer. Ancient rage,
its outlet abandoned, became molten,
a raw, red pair of lips like a girl's mouth
puffed in terror at having to pretend
she can predict the future and knows the truth
behind the mysterious responsibility
of her new job which she cannot learn
(it is too hard and hurts too much to be
alone and wrong). A ruptured core burns.
Drugged by Haldol in a darkened room,
my mother's job is the job of death.
Grow another mouth. Take another breath.

## YES

What awful thing will I take on
because you've asked? I can't say no.
Too hard to ask? It's only one
more awful thing that I'll take on
and do it all until it's gone,
except the thing will never go.
What awful thing will I take on
because you've asked? I can't say no.

# NO

Nothing grows a callus without a rub,
the constant irritation, then the raw,
red, leaking blister in response. The Law
of Skin is: eventual callus. Now scrub
any stain on the world with your hands!
While the callous response seems unfeeling,
it's only that the feeling
is done. And out of your hands.

# DOGGED PERSISTENCE

Slowly an armchair turns on some sort of pedestal.
Oh Mother I know you will be in it!
I'm here in the fog and vapors, waiting
for you, clear little eyes behind horn-rims,
to look up from your newspaper and stare out
at me, at me! But what a cold look you give.
You do not want to be bothered. *Mom,* I whisper,
*it's me.* You seem to have a reading lamp
—is that the little glow in the shrouded dimness?
"Don't bother me, Molly." Did you say that?
But I am searching for you! "Leave me alone."
Need, a child's need, a chill airless
panic instead of a mother as your chair
turns its back, and my hands dangle in the cold.
Where are you? You have to be out there somewhere.
I'll find you, I'll find you—how gray the sky is,
the sun a smothered 40-watt bulb behind clouds.
It is snowing, the sky decomposing,
each crystal, as we've all learned, individual,
as each person throughout millennia
is never replicated the same way,
yet out of the millions I will find the one
that is you. I have to.

# THE FARE

Bury me in my pink pantsuit, you said—and I did.
But I'd never dressed you before! I saw the glint
of gold in your jewelry drawer and popped
the earrings in a plastic bag along with pearls,
a pink-and-gold pin, and your perfume. ("What's this?"
the mortician said . . . "Oh well, we'll spray some on.")
Now your words from the coffin: *Take my earrings off!*
*I've had them on all day, for God's sake!"*
You've had them on five days. The lid's closed,
and the sharp stab of a femininity
you couldn't stand for more than two hours in life
is eternal—you'll never relax. I'm four hundred miles away.
Should I call up the funeral home and have them removed?
You're not buried yet—stored till the ground thaws—
where, I didn't ask. Probably the mortician's garage.
I should have buried you in slippers and a bathrobe.
Instead, I gave them your shoes. Oh, please
do it for me. I can't stand the thought of you
pained by vanity forever. Reach your cold hand
up to your ear and pull and hear the click
of the clasp hinge unclasping, then reach
across your face and get the other one
and—this effort could take you days, I know,
since you're dead. Let it be your last effort:
to change my mistake and be dead in comfort.
Lower your hands in their places
on your low mound of stomach and rest, rest,

you can let go of the earrings. They'll fall
to the bottom of the casket like tokens,
return fare fallen to the pit
of a coat's satin pocket.

# MISS, MISS, ARE YOU AWAKE?

What real flowers are these fake ones made to be?
Floppy peach heads, rapt on green wires, reach up
to the customers who slide into the booth
(gray leatherette, slow waitress, tea in a pot).
To love their copy natures is to love
by remembering what has come down to you
—for whatever it came *from* is long gone.
They are the embalmed versions, the mummies,
swaddled in cloth by painstaking hands
who reconstruct each stamen, pistil, petiole,
like morticians. My mother loved them.
"Doesn't she look beautiful?" her friends said
as they slid by to stare at her coffin,
the same as they'd say in a tearoom like this,
"Doesn't it look beautiful?" As I stopped here
on my way to the hospital, from the hospital,
to the apartment, from the empty apartment,
three hours each way through snow, I stopped
being repelled by cheap imitation,
understanding it's what I have, like
the lipsticked corpse that didn't really look
like her. Now I look at the flowers' faces,
unable to identify them either, and find
a welcome in their plumped satin centers
like the quilted satin in coffins. Before
the slow, slow waitress comes, I climb in.
Until I place my order, I'm wrapped on their stem.

*Friends and a Lover*

# UNSEEN

Behind this bamboo screen in my underwear
I watch my friend feed her parrots on the porch,
this and a floppy canvas shade our only wall,

about the thickness of a mainsail. Here
two dogs and a handy man join her, while I eat lunch
in a solitude as naked as a bathroom stall.

From this planned, reciprocal ignorance
she makes a kindness more intense than touch,
since it is actual touch withheld.

I am a sea she lowers her shade to, much
as she loves a vista, and in the new innocence
she leaves me to, feel closely held.

She's even got the dogs not to bother me,
and the birds mute in their makeshift tree.

# FLORAL CONVERSATION

Bursting with news—which friend to tell it to?
Neurotic, exciting, and morally
questionable—the one you choose will have to
tolerate you in a bad light. Corollary?
Pick one who loves ambiguity. Choosing
her hands and face, like petal and leaf, the skin
to photosynthesize your news, refusing
the shadow you cast yourself in, kin
to your enthusiasms, like a blue
delphinium next to a speckled foxglove
whispering in the garden—all this you
are bursting to find: someone to love
for liking you. As with two in the midday garden,
one might shade the other from the glare,
altering your light by her presence there.

# I CONSIDER THE POSSIBILITY

Long-waisted, tender-skinned and, despite the gym,
love roll about the midriff above the leggy limbs
muscled into knots at each calf, "beautiful for your age"
—bend over naked from your waist and show your red half-
peach of cunt to me who has fumbled at my cage
trying key after key in the stuck door with a half-laugh
after each failure; let me lay the bone of my nose
on the peach flesh and lift up my mouth to the pit
as I reach my arms toward the inverted throes
of your breasts, and as I touch your orange nipple tips
know that all my life I've wanted only men
and now, dispossessed of my neglectful mother
who herself toyed with the choice of women,
and upon being merrily teased by my therapist
at the prospect of such a love affair (the male "other"
has never incited such laughter), let me touch your wrist
at the dinner table and begin the silly maneuver
that will lead me to hold your head, to smooth your
hair all back, as in going through keys at the door my wrist
finally turns tender side up as the lock untwists.

# VOGUE VISTA

Since each old scar on my face seems a stone pillar
sunk below now tiered and gardened gradations,
discovering that caves of ruins were filler
in the making of this villa's new foundations
seems a natural progression toward this elegant
fête where you, my former love, my ex-founder, are bent
toward the opalescent skin below the eyes
of a Roman beauty. Your self-satisfied
sound of expansion to her flutter-laughter jars
the settings down the long table to where I am seated
between bored merchants. What I feel makes me
despair of what I feel: she is of god. Depleted
in my own planned vista, hurt and angry,
I am so human all I make is from a dying world.
You are a child in her goddess arms twirled.
Her face is a caper furled in its flower.
My hands fly batlike to my scars.

# PORTRAYAL

Hearing about a friend's friend over years,
not meeting that person perhaps for years,
then only at a social occasion
where both of you awkwardly need to shun
the intimacies you've near-feasted on,
is like the view from still lifes hung
on opposite sides of a gallery wall:
she the rabbit carcass strung upside down,
surrounded by cherries, lemons, and bowls;
you the trout splayed on blue-and-white towels
with grapes and eggs. Both of you are painted
by your friend's art, your connection created
by your own secrets inside the framed
flay which resembles you, beside her name.

# LOVE BEAT

How hard I try to kill my love,
its layered substance rank with strength,
appalling in its thickness, knotted as tree roots,
its muscle burled from running from the ax, its length
unmeasurable, for it contracts, footlike,
its tortoise pedal when touched. Its rhubarb stems
and burdock leaves make new love moot,
for my love now is old love, rude-barbed,
a prize vegetable in its prickered bed,
an animal as it thrives.
And the amount of blood that keeps it alive!
I know, for I've spilled it as I've chopped
with my ax at its inscrutable head
and seen its brain regenerate unrobbed,
while its love beat beats unstopped.

# THE HUNT

The stubby black-jowled dog inside me growls
and drools and warns and plants its crooked feet,
legs quivering, brindle chest staunched, and howls
until approachers back off in defeat,
although a brilliant poacher sometimes cows
my dog, my heart, its bitten hope, with meat,
flung viscera my tamed dog mauls
and then protects, well guarding what I eat
while poacher raises rifle: he follows
my deer into my wood, calling me dear, fleet
beauty, and I run, wholly my wild soul,
while the dumb, bristled dog I too am prowls,
guarding empty gate and empty street
till hunter becomes me, and we repeat.

# THE EXPLANATION

I won't explain since you can't understand,
nor would I expect you to climb inside
the jewelled crater of my skull and stand
among the ruins, scout among them, then hide

from me, your enemy, inside my own terrain,
crystallized from previous blows—not all yours.
Nor will I now expect you to refrain
from assessment as you stand outdoors,

canvassing my geode skull's smooth surface
and, seeing no clues as to the damage
or to the quirky beauty of old ravage,
urge me again and again to confess

that because I'm hard and hidden from you
you're forced to hysterics from nothing to do.

## BAUBLES AFTER BOMBS

Little metal symbols gambol in the bright
pastures of the cases—the world in sight
for a moment, coincidences hinged
together in a genuine plan, parts phalanged
as finger joints, clasped and ringed
in the jewelry display. Elsewhere someone's job
is picking arms and fingers from war rubble,
while we pick out our pins, one a cat's head—
it doesn't look severed at all. Meant to be
displayed with turquoise eyes that do not sob,
chin a perfect end to its body. . . . Rubble-
searching for human debris is all our job, bent
on recovering as we are, so in this case we see
our hopes made gold facts. Beauty in a world sacked
is whimsy's rearrangement of organs and limbs,
all things in miniature akin: a frog's head,
a dog's head, gemmed hearts chained to a pin.

*Prayers and Reasons*

# RELIGIOUS INSTRUCTION

No fires are built (except spiritual ones)
in the rectory fireplace, full of philodendrons
which stare directly out at the orphans

(grown-up ones) seated in front of them. Father
sits to one side with Bonnie the dog super-
vising the group of two whose spirits stir

slowly. It's cold in here: stewed tea, winter rain,
sweaters, prayer books, questions almost restrained,
then asked awkwardly, revealing a naked moraine

of bald rocks and dirt left by glaciers receding
somewhere in these two women alternately reading
the Creed aloud, in their mourning needing

(Bonnie yawns, but the priest, amused and stern,
a widower himself, insists that they learn
to walk the scaffolds of the Trinity to mourn

what smashed so far below) . . . needing what?
A Heavenly Parent now that the real ones are gone. Cut
like paper dolls from the tall city's book, they've shut,

with effort, the heavy rectory door to sit with a priest
and his dog in the dead of winter where at least
a fire might be lit in the fireplace for Christ's

sake. Instead the hearth is filled with greens,
a houseplant arrangement in homely baskets: green
fire. Father explains what everything means.

But what *does* everything mean? The collie yawns,
mouth wide open, her foul breath a wind that spawns
migrations across imaginary lawns

—green fire—to the other side, into God's mirth.
Can these three orphans laugh on earth?
Dog thumps tail on hearth.

Can they take themselves lightly?
What can the rough stone rectory rectify?
Less than weighs on them nightly.

How pleasant, now that they are man and women, to obey,
saying what they were taught to say
now that the work week is over, and it's Saturday

when thought roams in daydream, which is thought's right,
ranging, leash dangling, for the ritual words unknot
what was tied, and what was intolerable is not.

# IN A LONG LINE OF HORSES

Sweet tang of horse at dry edge of canyon,
steep tiny path descends, as subway stairs
descend through platforms in complex stations.
Clumsy, citified, never ridden a mare,
never been to a canyon of deep urban architecture
unearthed by celestial hands and turned to light,
man-made become god-made. God's maid I am,
thrilled to look agoraphobically down to the right:
drop to death immediate. "Don't lean, ma'am,"
the cowboy says. I straighten, of course,
and think with sudden pleasure of the animal below,
scratch her ears, and talk to her, though all
she loves is her chapped angel, the cowboy.
They lead hundreds into the canyon. We each enjoy
a superficial blue moment on her back. As pilgrims
we are not individuals in control. Her whim
to throw us may be her inner call. To trust
that she will do her work is our work
as we follow the stations of the canyon thrust
into our saddles against good city reason.
Where is the train? We are the train.

# SUBWAY VESPERS

Thank you for some ventilation and a pole for my hands.
Thank you that the man with whiskey breath and
bloodshot eyes, business suit, plus monogrammed

cuffs (likely to behave) is significantly
taller than I am, leaving me inches of free
space between my place at the pole, his, and the lady

weeping below me. Over the loudspeaker a voice
informs us a track obstruction leaves no choice
but for a man to check each car's wheels twice.

Obstruction? Must be a body. Try to see:
nothing but black tunnel walls and the guilty
heads of those with seats. Thank you for my dusty clothes,

and that we are not naked in a cattle car.
After they find the body, we won't have to walk far.
A man's legs dangle above the door . . .

but he's alive, mumbling into his beeper.
The conductor replies on the loudspeaker,
"Only garbage on the track!" You, our keeper,

we thank you for releasing the brake.
We'll go home, buyers of fish, bread, and steak,
to sit and watch the news we do not make.

The engine starts. My prayer implodes with a red
shot of relief that we won't be led
down a tunnel, past a corpse, out from the track bed,
but delivered to a lighted station instead.

# SIMPLE

When the wafer dissolves on my tongue I won-
der what part of the Lord I have eaten,
His scrotum molecularly recon-
structed in a pale disc, or a wheaten
flap of armpit? Perhaps internal organs
vaporized to universal atoms
from the thorax of our Lord. Others had plans
to preserve the saints in bits, the phantom
of Anthony's larynx in a ruby vase,
Agatha's breasts in gold caskets, the flesh
reserved. I only eat our Lord and mas-
ticate the host, the church a crèche,
and I in my stall not even knowing how
to blow glass housing for a saint or wield
a hammer with my hoof, unable to bow
or scoop breasts into a box. The world
transubstantiates me to animal
evolving in reverse: soon I could be a lizard
on the wall of the manger, in time one-celled,
perhaps a single cell of the baby Lord,
perhaps His tongue, so what I chew as symbol
I might at last become: simple.

# FORGIVENESS

Forgiveness is not an abstraction for
it needs a body to feel its relief.
Knees, shoulders, spine are required to adore
the lightness of a burden removed. Grief,
like a journey over water completed,
slides its keel in the packed sand reef.
Forgiveness is contact with the belief
that your only life must now be lived. Knees
once sank into the leather of the pew with all
the weight of created hell, of whom you did not ease,
or what you did not seize. Now the shortfall
that crippled your posture finds sudden peace
in the muscular, physical brightness
of a day alive: the felt lightness
of existence self-created, forgiveness.

# CANCELLED ELEGY

Draw a bath without bubbles. Warm water
with a slightly yellowish cast. (Imagine
life as a window to itself.) No food for
two days before—all evacuated. Sin
to let a big mess spoil it. (Your bowels go
into spasm when you die.) Step in. Put
your head back on the ledge. Place the blade so
it's easily reached. When relaxed and warm, cut
across each wrist beneath the water's skin
and let blood flow like the ancient Romans.
But doesn't a bath defy self-denial?
Clear, but unlike glass, it laps. Nothing
can be cut from it. There is your frail
body in the tub's womb, where you feel pain,
my darling thing, because you feel warm.

## HAPPY BIRTHDAY

Whenever I feel I am most myself,
a baking cake welled up beyond its pan
is what I am, anchored, yet uncontained. The gulf
I feel whenever I am most myself
between my sides and insides on the oven shelf
overflowing, like words outpouring, not by plan,
is itself the me I am when I am most myself:
a cake out loud! its mouth the pan.

# UPBRINGING

Bringing yourself up requires long hours alone
to get the nurturing others have felt.
Because of someone else, others have grown up,

so they question why your solitude has grown
so wide, and you wonder at your guilt
that simply being requires these hours alone

with your obstreperous, largely unknown
Being, who only feels and doesn't talk,
whose matted, scaly pelt you've sewn

into what you hope is proper clothing, stock-
still, costumed in a darkness that never melts.
Of course you must take it out when it moans

and let it be naked and chew the bones
and hooves you save for it, after it bolts
around the room and falls, exhausted, down

into the possessed happiness of its selfhood.
This takes hours. As if holding your breath underwater,
you hold in the aboriginal child, attending to the *om*

society seems to breathe that you, a clone,
never seem to understand until you're sick
from something vomiting inside its false home,

and the child feels it's done wrong although
it's only an animal. Now you must clean up alone
or you'll both be sick, or one of you will die.

Of course this takes the hours most spend on the phone,
making money, having kids,
or asking why you don't.

# GOOD-BYE HELLO IN THE EAST VILLAGE
*1993*

Three tables down from Allen Ginsberg we sit
in JJ's Russian Restaurant. My old friend,
who's struggled for happiness, insists
on knowing why I'm happy. An end
to my troubles of the century? *"Listen, Molly, if I*
*didn't know you so well, I'd think you were*
*faking this good cheer,"* she says, her eyes
bright openings like a husky's eyes in its fur.
(My friend is half an orphan. It's cold in here.)
The East Village shuffles past JJ's window,
and we hear Allen order loudly in the ear
of the waitress, *"Steamed only! No cholesterol!"*
"I could tell you it's my marriage, Nita,
and how much I love my new life in two countries,
but the real reason," I beam irresistibly at a
dog walker with 8 dogs on leashes in the freezing
evening outside JJ's window where we sit,
"is that I'm *an orphan*. It's *over.* They're
*both* dead." Her lids narrow her eyes to a slit
of half-recognition. "I couldn't say this,"—there!
the waitress plunks two bowls of brilliant magenta
borscht, pierogi, and hunks of challah
—"to just *anybody,"*—jewel heaps of food on Formica
—only to you, who wouldn't censure me,
since you've witnessed me actually fantasize
chopping their heads from their necks from their limbs
to make a soup of the now dead Them to feed
the newly happily alive Me.

An old order is dimmed,
just as the U.S., its old enemy
the U.S.S.R. vaporized, disarms itself,
nearly wondering what a century's fuss
was all about . . . what *was* my fuss about?
But even a struggle to the death is levelled
in the afterlife of relief. A bevel
in the glass of America has connected
along a strip of this life to the window
of JJ's restaurant connecting Nita and me, wed
to the nightlife on Second Avenue, though
in reflection only, the reflection that now perfectly
joins Ginsberg with his steamed vegetables
and us with our steamy borscht and pierogi
to the ice-pocked sidewalk, God's table,
full of passersby, pointing occasionally to Allen,
joined now by an Asian boy, but more often
just hurrying past in the cold as we eat
the food of a previous enemy
and find it brightly delicious—*it is meet
and right so to do*—in the world now ours,
the century's hours hurtling behind
like snow-wake off an empty dogsled.
Old friends, we rest, not talking, well fed,
since at this cold dark moment things are fine.

# MATINS

Rain hisses off the bus and car and taxi tires,
hosing the almost gardened streets; blackened lanes
of traffic seem planned as garden paths;
buildings wired like cemented topiaries
lean into their baths, and it's spring,
we're alive, the city a human-made Eden,
so gray, not green, though there in the fruit stands
jonquils and hyacinths bow in tin buckets and
figures in slickers duck out to shop, a wet parade
of flower heads conveyed along below.
It occurs to me to pray.
In a little seizure, a prayer shudders up,
its spasm quick as a camera's shutter:
*Glad you exist to rise up, window.*

# PRAIRIE PRAYER

Time rolls out like a prairie.
Do not be afraid.
The mind forms a prayer
from endless land's creed.

The straight-blade horizon
is grass blades in billions,
silver slanted in the sun,
the prairie soft bullion

beyond stamp or use,
unowned, undone, unformed.
A prayer forms alone
when time undoes, unforms.

The self, like land itself,
beyond stamp or use
in its unfarmed wealth,
telescopes into the mind.

Now, if the mind had fingers
it would touch its thought.
Such contact would be prayer,
an endless plain inside there.

# LIFE STUDY

Take a blank page and from the bottom draw
a line to the midpoint: now you have depth.
This is perspective. The line is distance.
In life that line is healing. It causes terror
to abrade. Why won't my memory try to draw
3-dimensional pain on a tablet's page?
Because healing moves memory into day.
Fully lighted, kindnesses appear to repay
some of the old debts. Now faces are appealing
and complex, their angles jumping into relief.
Now real rain enlivens vistas from the depths
of hopes deserted at too young an age. Trauma
redistributes its colors, old drama quelled
to tables laid for meals, now actually eaten.
You could say I've whitewashed my youth, since light
from the end of the tunnel washes back through:
as I draw I see not what I stumbled through,
but each illumined site.

# WHY I AM NOT A BUDDHIST

I love desire, the state of want and thought
of how to get; building a kingdom in a soul
requires desire. I love the things I've sought—
you in your beltless bathrobe, tongues of cash that loll
from my billfold—and love what I want: clothes,
houses, redemption. Can a new mauve suit
equal God? Oh no, desire is ranked. To lose
a loved pen is not like losing faith. Acute
desire for nut gateau is driven out by death,
but the cake on its plate has meaning,
even when love is endangered and nothing matters.
For my mother, health; for my sister, bereft,
wholeness. But why is desire suffering?
Because want leaves a world in tatters?
How else but in tatters should a world be?
A columned porch set high above a lake.
Here, take my money. A loved face in agony,
the spirit gone. Here, use my rags of love.

# Index of Titles

# Index of First Lines

# About the Author

Molly Peacock, poet-in-residence at Poet's Corner, the Cathedral of St. John the Divine, divides her time between New York and Toronto. She is President Emerita of the Poetry Society of America and one of the originators of *Poetry in Motion,* the popular program of placards on subways and buses. A Woodrow Wilson Fellow as well as Lecturer at the Unterberg Poetry Center, 92nd Street Y, Peacock has been a writer-in-residence at numerous colleges and universities, including the University of Toronto's Taddle Creek Workshops. Her prose works include *How to Read a Poem . . . and Start a Poetry Circle* and *Paradise, Piece by Piece.* She is the editor of the anthology, *The Private I: Privacy in a Public World.* Molly Peacock is married to Michael Groden, a Joyce scholar.